THE LOW-CARB VEGAN COOKBOOK

Ketogenic Breads, Fat Bombs & Delicious Plant-Based Recipes

By Eva Hammond
Version 1.1
Published by HMPL Publishing at KDP

*Find us at **happyhealthygreen.life***

INTRODUCTION

Welcome to the ultimate guide to discovering the best recipes and nutritional information that caters to not only one, but two, dietary lifestyles! Here you will be able to effortlessly browse through a directory of endless recipes accommodating both a ketogenic and a vegan diet, better known as the ketogenic vegan diet, also referred to as a low carb, high-fat vegan (LCHF vegan).

At first glance the ketogenic vegan diet may seem to be a bit contradictory. We are taking the ketogenic diet, a more scientific approach towards our health and optimum energy by consuming minimal carbohydrates and focusing on fat rich foods, and combining it with the vegan diet, a health-based diet that originally stems from the moral of consuming no animal product, which means a high carb, low-fat diet. For people who are unaware of the vegan diet, let me give a brief introduction. A vegan diet is one that does not include meat. Not only that, it completely excludes any form of dairy products such as eggs or milk products.

Despite allegations that Veganism is not a healthy lifestyle, the vegan diet has proven to be a healthy one over the years. It includes almost every color in the rainbow including fruits, vegetables, legumes, beans and grains. The list is as infinite as the number of dishes that can be made by combining the above foods.

Ironically, people usually associate the keto diet with a focus on animal fats and the vegan diet with just the opposite. That's what makes this combination so interesting: following a ketogenic vegan diet not only allows you the freedom and peace of mind that comes with a cruelty-free vegan diet, but also the high nutritional levels that come with the ketogenic diet.

This is where you might pause and ask yourself: "So I just got my hands on a book that is going to give me amazing nutritional information and delicious, mouth-watering recipes, and they are completely kind to my body and all sentient beings around me?!" That's exactly what this is, and it is only once people begin educating themselves and look into adopting this lifestyle and dietary path that they will realize how excruciatingly simple it all really is. Yes, you can get the best of both worlds. Sacrifice life? Sacrifice health? Sacrifice taste? No. Why have we put it in our minds that it is just not possible to simultaneously satisfy all of these categories? At the end of the day, we all deserve, not to mention are *allowed*, to satisfy all of our food-related wants in a guilt-free manner, and now that you know it is 100% possible, why not?!

Ultimately, as mentioned above, the ketogenic vegan diet combines two diets that would originally seem to be at opposite ends of the spectrum. Many people's first thoughts on it may be along the lines of this metaphor: Imagine this combination diet as a Venn-diagram, with one circle representing the ketogenic diet, and the other representative of the vegan diet. The small section in the middle created by the overlapping of both circles would represent the combined, compromised views of the ketogenic vegan diet. My point being that, when initially thought about, people may assume that the options of the two "limited" diets get even more restricted to satisfy both diet's perspectives; however, this is merely a misconception. The ketogenic vegan diet extols just the opposite by unlocking the gateways to endless possibilities of wholesome, fresh foods. You know all the unnecessary filler aisles in your local grocery store consisting of processed foods, "fresh" flesh, or animal based dairy that were originally considered to be the endless "options" we were being restricted from when accepting the keto vegan diet? Well, each of those categories should have never really been considered options at all. Thus, what is left in the middle of this "Venn-diagram" is what should have been there from the start: real food.

This book will serve as your handy, detailed guide to how to begin going about the combination of these two moral and dietary spheres. Are you ready for the best of each world without having to sacrifice a single thing? It is possible, and we are here to show you how!

So how can you combine those two worlds?

You are going to minimize the carbohydrates you eat by ensuring all of the veggies and fruits you consume are on the lower end of the sugar scale. And on the flip side, you will enjoy all sorts of delicious vegan fats like those found in avocados and buttery nuts. And no, you don't have to do any of the guesswork; we've calibrated all of the recipes for you so you will watch the pounds slide off while your energy increases and you feel better than you have ever felt before.

We have included delicious recipes from Spicy Spinach Quiche to Pumpkin Pie Bites and everything in between. You're going to love the flavors, and these dishes will fill you up while keeping you in a ketogenic state so your body is constantly burning fat. The dishes are also quite simple to make and you don't need a lot of fancy ingredients.

Again, a simple way to eat clean is to stay away from a good majority of the aisles at your grocery store, which are often filled with junk foods that give you a load of calories without any of the nutritional benefits that a calorie is supposed to bring. (But remember this excludes your go-to aisles that contain dried nuts and fruits!) When you're eating vegan you're eating plant-based and that means you are eating all natural, all green and all good for your body and the environment.

In terms of health and nutrition, the vegan diet is completely free of cholesterol and saturated animal fat. Plant-based foods don't have high amounts of cholesterol. Cholesterol is primarily found in animal products like eggs, dairy and meat. Studies have shown that vegan diets tend to have lower levels of cholesterol in general. Cholesterol is not a bad thing nor is it particularly good either. On a low carb, high fat eating plan you may actually increase your HDL (the good cholesterol for the body) by consuming more saturated fats. Because of this, vegans are less likely to develop heart disease, type 2 diabetes, high blood pressure, and some forms of cancer.

Meat has many more calories and fat than plant food options. Which means it's more likely for you to be overweight if you are eating the higher fat food options, like meat and meat products. Nutritionists cite numerous studies showing people that eat meat as a staple in their diet are ten times more likely to be overweight than vegans. Add to that the fact that meat eaters also show a lifelong trend of gaining more weight as the years tick by.

In other words, it's safe to say opting for healthy vegan eating will help you slim down for life. When you need to lose weight, it is very unwise for you to adopt a fad diet that contains less nutrients and is low in fat. It will make your body feel deprived. A vegan diet is a healthy option containing foods such as olive oil, seeds, nuts and avocados.

Losing weight happens when your calorie expenditure exceeds your calorie intake. That means you either eat less or exercise more. In general, it's easier to reduce your intake.

When practicing a keto vegan diet, another concern is achieving ketosis. This is a metabolic process in which, with insufficient carbs to burn for energy, your body will burn fat instead. It occurs when you eat a diet high in healthy fats and low in carbohydrates.

As a side effect of this process, ketones are created. Once you start your keto vegan diet, you can buy test strips to check the amount of ketones in your blood or urine, thereby finding out whether or not you are in ketosis. You can get into ketosis in as little as one to two days.

Please consult with your doctor before attempting to go into ketosis if you have any particular concerns, especially if you are diabetic, have high blood pressure, or are pregnant or breastfeeding.

If you ever want to increase your calories or fat ratio, add some coconut oil or olive oil to your meals. You can also try eating a few nuts or adding a spoonful of flax seed or hemp seed to a meal. Increasing the amount of healthy fats, you consume will also keep you feeling fuller longer. You may actually feel less hungry even though you're eating less than before.

More energy and improved mental focus are other possible benefits. This diet is also excellent for building and maintaining muscle. Many weight lifters and bodybuilders swear by the keto diet, a growing number of which prefer a keto vegan diet.

TABLE OF CONTENTS

DISCLAIMER

The recipes provided in this report are for informational purposes only and are not intended to provide dietary advice. A medical practitioner should be consulted before making any changes in diet. Additionally, recipe cooking times may require adjustment depending on age and quality of appliances. Readers are strongly urged to take all precautions to ensure Ingredients are fully cooked in order to avoid the dangers of food borne viruses. The recipes and suggestions provided in this book are solely the opinion of the author. The author and publisher do not take any responsibility for any consequences that may result due to following the instructions provided in this book.

BONUS

Welcome to the reader's circle of happyhealthygreen.life.
You can subscribe to our newsletter using this link:
http://happyhealthygreen.life/vegan-newsletter

By subscribing to our newsletter, you will receive the latest vegan recipes, tips about health & nutrition and plant-based cooking articles that make your mouth water, right in your inbox.

We also offer you a unique opportunity to read future vegan cookbooks for absolutely free...

Get your hands on free vegan recipes and instant access to 'The Vegan Cookbook'. **Subscribe** to the vegan newsletter and grab your free copy here at:
http://happyhealthygreen.life/vegan-newsletter

Enter your email address to get instant access.
Support veganism and say NO to animal cruelty!
We don't like spam and understand you don't like spam either.
We'll email you no more than 2 times per week.

WHAT IS THE KETOGENIC DIET?

When you eat, your body breaks down all the carbohydrates present in the food into glucose. This glucose is what acts as fuel for your everyday functioning. The idea behind the ketogenic diet is to reduce the number of carbohydrates and force the body to enter the ketosis state. It is a state in which the body burns its fat instead of the carbs that you take in. The process starts when your liver releases ketones. The primary purpose of the ketogenic diet is to encourage your body to stop burning carbs as fuel and instead burn fat as ketones. This process is achieved by lowering the level of carb intake to 50 grams per day.

But what is ketosis? Ketosis is a metabolic process where the production of ketones by the liver is undertaken. What usually happens when the intake of carbohydrates is lowered is that the body adjusts and shifts into ketosis. A high percentage of cells in the human body utilizes ketones as a source of energy. The usage of ketone usually occurs at a time of long fast or restricted consumption of carbohydrates. Ketones can provide energy for most organs in the body. It is very important to know that glucose is the primary energy provider for most cells in the body. For the purpose of conserving energy for future use, the body stores excess glucose as glycogen. This glycogen is found in the liver and in the muscles. The glycogen stored in the liver is used to maintain normal levels of glucose in the blood. In contrast, glycogen that has been stored up in the muscles is for the purpose of fueling muscle activities. When carbohydrate intake restriction is in high gear, protein, as well as fats, can be used as a source of energy. The majority of cells in the body can make use of fatty acids for energy. In a time of shortage or complete lack of carbohydrates, the liver breaks down fat. At such times, ketone bodies can be used by most cells. The production of ketones in excess of what the body requires makes the level of ketones increase resulting in what is known as ketosis.

The key thing to remember is that if you are not following the ketogenic diet to perfection, it will lead to a number of medical situations. For instance, your body can produce too many ketones in uncontrolled diabetes making you ill. Therefore, whenever you are following a ketogenic diet, it is imperative that you follow it correctly.

Your body is responsible for thousands of operations at any given second. Right there you blinked, breathed, your body is digesting your last meal and it's doing all of these things without you having to think about it. So you can imagine that your body is quite busy and it's going to try to do things with as little effort as possible.

The average person's diet consists of carbohydrates, protein and fat. Carbohydrates are super easy for your body to break down and use for energy, but proteins and fats are more difficult. When you eat a meal, your body is going to use the carbohydrates right away. Proteins are usually used for other functions like muscle maintenance so the body doesn't use them for energy. Finally, fat is more difficult to breakdown than sugar so the body uses it as a last resource.

So when you eat carbohydrates and fats together, the body uses the carbs and stores the fat. If you don't get enough carbs in your diet, the body will start to use the fat because it has to – and this is when your body goes into a ketogenic state. A ketogenic state simply means your body is using fat for energy – and that is great news for anyone trying to get lean.

In order for you to get your body to burn fat for fuel instead of carbohydrates, you need to feed your body low carbs and more fat. In addition, the carbs you eat should be complex carbs instead of simple carbs because complex carbs are also difficult for your body to breakdown. Complex carbs are found in veggies, whole grains, beans and lentils. Carbs that are difficult for your body to break down require more energy so when you eat them, they require more energy to break down and the body will turn to fats to get more of that energy.

When you reduce your carbohydrate intake, your body has no choice but to start using fats for energy and that is when you enter the ketogenic state. The ketogenic state is also known as the fat burning state because it is when your body doesn't have enough carbohydrates to use for energy so it uses fats.

Why eating more fat means burning more fat

When you eat a high amount of carbohydrates you will feel sluggish because your body uses the carbs quickly and then you have no energy left. But when you consume fats, it takes longer for your body to break them down into energy so you are fed a steady amount of fat energy as your body breaks down the fat molecules. This also means you feel fuller longer and so have no need to reach for harmful snacks.

You must understand that your body has a lot of work to do so it is going to try to make that as easy as possible. If you feed it a ton of carbohydrates, it will use these carbohydrates for energy and will always store your fat. But if you get rid of the carbs then your body will burn your fat – it is as simple as that!

WHAT IS VEGANISM

Veganism goes beyond a diet. It is a lifestyle choice and one that people make with a fair amount of consideration to not just their own bodies but also the effect their choices are making in the world.

A vegan diet is focused on plant-based food and all animal consumption is eliminated. The difference between vegetarianism and veganism is that, although vegetarians will consume animal products like eggs and milk, vegans will not.

The choice to go vegan is a personal one, one that goes far beyond food consumption. One of the core reasons individuals decide to go vegan is because they no longer want to participate in a practice that harms animals. Another big reason for switching to a vegan lifestyle is that many people believe that the human body was not designed to consume animals. And since the body was not designed to consume animals, it doesn't have the tools to break down animal products in a good way - which is harmful to the body.

Once the decision has been made to follow a vegan diet, there are some very important things people must think about when it comes to the food they're eating. Since an animal-based diet provides most of the nutrients a person needs, most of us don't think about the individual nutrients we need. Going vegan means you must be conscious of the types of foods you are eating to ensure you are getting everything your body needs.

One of the biggest concerns about turning to veganism is your amino acid consumption. You can get all the amino acids you need when you eat meat products, but when it comes to plant-based foods, you must get a mix of the right foods together to get all the amino acids your body must have.

What are amino acids?

Amino acids are the building blocks of your body, the ones that help form your muscle and tissue and so they are essential. Your body can form some amino acids on its own, but for others you have to get them from outside sources. There are 9 amino acids that are essential for optimal function which your body cannot create; they are methionine, leucine, isoleucine, histidine, lysine, phenylalanine, tryptophan, valine, and threonine. It is easy to get the complete nine amino acids from animal products but to get such from vegan products you have to combine various foods.

Combining simple things like beans and quinoa is enough to make a complete protein. You have to remember that you don't need to get all the essential amino acids from one food, you can get them from combining foods throughout your day. So being vegan does not mean you lose any nutritional value, it means only that you have to make sure you are eating a variety of foods. Doing this will ensure you are getting all the amino acids your body requires.

Amino acids (AA) will bond together to form peptides or polypeptides. From there, the proteins are made. Your body requires 20 different kinds of amino acids to create proteins. Each type determines what the shape will be like when formed.

There are essential and non-essential amino acids that exist today. Some of them are present in your body while others cannot be synthesized, thus, they need to be obtained from food.

Essential amino acids perform critical functions in your body. For instance, in order to obtain normal sleep, you will need certain amino acids. They can also reduce anxiety and depression and make your immune system stronger.

Amino acids make up 75% of your body. Every bodily function depends on them. Every chemical reaction happening within your body relies on the proteins formed from their bond.

Their volume is considered to be the most common type in the human body. Hence, every human being, plant or animal depends on them to survive.

These essential amino acids must be ingested every day. If you fail to supply your body with enough of them, it could lead to protein degradation. This is because your system does not store them in your body like fats, starches, etc.

The good thing is that amino acids are found in nature. You can obtain them from diverse sources like microorganisms and plants, among others.

You can also take food and dietary supplements that contain amino acids. They are proven to offer health benefits such as decreasing your risk of developing life-threatening medical conditions and improving your energy levels each day.

Your body needs amino acids to develop and repair muscle and organ tissue. They are also essential in the production of hormones and enzymes. Your hair, skin, teeth and nails need amino acids for proper growth. They can also generate antibodies to help in defending against infection. Essentially, they maintain the overall growth of your body and control its metabolic functions.

You may think that those categorized as non-essential amino acids are not important in your bodily functions. Although the term non-essential is misleading, amino acids that fall into this category are still extremely important. They cannot be produced without the essential amino acids. So, in a way, they are still influenced by diet.

After you consume protein, your body digests and metabolizes the protein to produce amino acids. Then, the amino acids produced are utilized by the system to generate different cell types and chemical compounds.

In order to maintain proper levels of amino acids, you need to maintain a balanced diet, which is required for overall health and fitness.

The levels of amino acids in your body are constant. They do not depend on your diet. Then again, your body tends to attack itself by breaking down muscle and other tissues in order to keep the amino acids' concentration level.

How to ensure you have enough energy on a vegan diet

As you travel down the vegan roadway, you will want to be careful that you are getting enough calories in your diet since all calories are not made equal and certainly not the calories you get from animal products versus vegetable products. A cup of veggies is not going to give you the same energy or nutrients that a cup of meat would. A cup of almonds will give you a lot more fat.

Consult an Expert

It is also important that you consult your doctor before you make such a drastic change in your diet. One of the major challenges for individuals is to replace what they are missing when not consuming animal products. Vitamins like B12 can only be found in meat products and many people end up taking supplements to make up for a lack of B12. You can determine with your health professional what the best choice is for you, but the most important thing is that you are getting everything you need to function at your best.

Understanding the value of the energy you get from your carbs and fats is critical and we're here to help you do that. It isn't difficult to understand this and once you do, you'll be armed with the knowledge of life.

What exactly is B12 and how do vegans get it?

When many people hear of a vegan or vegetarian based diet, or any diet largely absent of "flesh foods" one of the first questions you might hear may be along the lines of "Aren't you going to have iron or vitamin deficiency? That's not healthy". Actually, with a bit of proper education, the above statement can be completely false. Following a wholesome, animal free diet may have a few initial challenges in the vitamin department. Some new vegans, vegetarians, or keto vegans may, in fact, initially struggle with their B12 levels, since it can only be found naturally in foods such as red meat, fish, crab and dairy related products. But with appropriate knowledge multiple healthy alternatives can always be identified.

A common misconception is that a meat and dairy free diet means never taking vitamins such as B12, which would lead to fatigue, iron deficiency, and unhealthy nerve and blood cells. The reason the above statement is believed by many to be true is that the B12 vitamin is one that is only found naturally in a majority of meat-related products as mentioned above. However, while that is true, B12 intake for people with accommodated dietary needs is in fact possible! Essentially, while daily intake levels for the B12 vitamin only reach 2.4 micrograms to 2.8 micrograms, consumption is extremely vital for the nutrients it provides your body with.

You'll be glad to hear that B12 is now found in multiple "fortified foods" (meaning foods that have been injected with certain nutrients) such as soy based dairy. In addition, if that's not up your alley, the B12 vitamin is even offered as gelatin free supplements.

Being knowledgeable of this information will allow you to jump into your dietary changes with no problems at all. At the end of the day, you can still be receiving all the nutrients you need with no harm done to you or any living being around you.

YOUR MACROS

Macronutrients are to the body what gasoline is to the gas-powered car. The 3 main macronutrients are protein, carbohydrates and fat; these three nutrients provide us with the energy we need to function. The three macronutrients are not created equal so each one provides a different amount of energy per serving. Most researchers have found that fats provide the most energy per serving compared to proteins and carbohydrates.

Protein

We are essentially walking protein, which means our hair, nails, muscles and organs are all made out of protein. Through complex biological processes, proteins are broken down into amino acids. These amino acids further break down into other compounds and become the basic tools our body needs to repair itself after the strain of daily life (or hard workouts.) Amino acids facilitate connections between neurons in our body and brain. Protein itself is broken down into amino acids, and our body is capable of making some amino acids, but not all that we require. Our body needs 20 amino acids and it can produce 11 of them, but the remaining 9 we have to get from food. Ingest too much protein and it becomes stored as glucose which, as we've seen already, is sugar that the body will then rely on for energy.

Protein is necessary for the body's and brain's development and function and the body uses a lot of it. If there isn't enough protein in the body, the body then starts taking it from your muscles so it is important to be steadily fueled with protein.

Good sources of keto vegan protein include tofu, nuts and seeds like flax and chia.

Carbohydrates

Carbohydrates are molecules made up of a combination of hydrogen, carbon and oxygen. Carbohydrates are a pre-ketogenic person's energy supply. They become glucose (sugar), which the body then uses for a boost. Unfortunately, that sugar rush releases insulin, which stockpiles glucose in the forms of both glycogen (a different kind of sugar) and fat cells. The ketogenic diet is designed to minimize carb-consumption and maximize burning of glucose, glycogen and fat. On this diet, your body is becoming far more efficient at processing.

The most common forms of carbohydrates are sugar, fiber and starch. Our body certainly needs some carbohydrates in the diet but most people consume carbohydrates in excess. Carb-rich foods are satisfying and usually inexpensive, which is one of the reasons they are consumed so readily. But carb-heavy foods are often void of the necessary nutrients. It is possible to get energy from carbs like white bread and soda pop, but these things don't have the nutrients you need. There is, however, a way to eat the right carbs that will give you what you need.

There are two types of carbohydrates – complex and simple. Simple carbohydrates, high-level Glycemic Index foods such as white bread or potatoes, are generally sugars and are easily broken down by the body and used right away causing a spike in your insulin levels. This means your blood sugar instantly soars for a short period of time, soon dropping back down, and you get hungry quite quickly after since the carb is rapidly used up. Complex carbohydrates are those that take your body a longer period of time to break down, thus being on the lower end of the Glycemic Index (which is best for helping your body efficiently metabolize fat). For example, eating a bowl of lentils, a low-level GI food, would allow you to have steady blood glucose levels, which in turn would keep you satiated longer, as well as significantly aid in the metabolizing of their fat levels. In summary, complex carbs take longer to break down so your blood glucose levels do not spike out of control and you feel fuller longer.

When you are eating carbohydrates you should ensure that you're getting most of yours from the complex carb family. This would mean that most of the carbs you are consuming would not be considered net carbs or, in other words, carbs that you are trying to decrease as much as possible. This means eating things like vegetables and whole grain while staying away from simple things like white sugar and white flour. However, if you are following a gluten-free regimen, you would probably opt for other great gluten-free fiber sources, such as lentils, beans, green peas and so on.

Fats

Over the past three decades it has been drilled into our minds that fat is bad – period. The truth of the matter, however, is that the body needs fat. For one, we need fat to absorb certain fat-soluble vitamins like A, D, E and K. Without fat the body is not able to absorb those much-needed vitamins. Additionally, we need fat for healthy skin and hair as well as a protective insulator.

Your body is unable to produce essential fatty acids so it is critical that you consume good fat sources. These essential fats help with numerous body processes like regulating blood pressure, protecting organs and brain development functions.

Consuming unsaturated fats is the best bet. Unsaturated fats are in a liquid state and generally come from plant sources. Saturated fats are solid and generally come from animal sources. Trans fats are a third major fat. These fats are more often than not produced by companies trying to increase the shelf life of their products. Trans fats are unsaturated fats that are turned into saturated fats by hydrogenizing the unsaturated fat. Needless to say, trans fats are super bad and should, in fact, be avoided.

Plant-based oils are a great Keto Vegan source of unsaturated fats. Butters like cocoa butter and coconut cream are also great sources of Keto Vegan fats. For added nutrition, there have been studies stating coconut oil is "overrated" as it only temporarily aids your body's nutritional levels. In fact, while coconut oil may claim to decrease LDL levels, in other words your bad cholesterol levels, it eventually adds to your LDL levels in the long run. As a result, while many recipes lean towards the use of coconut oil, remember that any oil of your choice works just as well. These include sunflower oil, flax seed oil, and olive oil, to name a few, which gives your body a well-balanced array of fats.

OMEGA 3-6-9

Fatty Acids are vital for your body's functions from your respiratory system to your circulatory system to your brain and other vital organs. Ultimately, while the body does produce fatty acids such as the Omega-9 fatty acid on its own for multiple different tasks, there are two essential fatty acids (EFA's) it does not produce: Omega-3 and Omega-6.

The Omega-3 Fatty Acid is responsible for aiding in brain function as well as preventing cardiovascular disease. This fatty acid prevents asthma, certain cancers, arthritis, high cholesterol, blood pressure and so on. Many say that our dosage of Omega-3 can be satisfied by consuming fatty fish such as salmon; however, it's a great misconception that vegans will lack this vital nutrient due to not being able to consume fatty-flesh foods. While Omega-3 is most popularly taken from fish, it has a plethora of different sources as well, including green vegetables, chia seed oil, flaxseed oils, raw walnuts and hempseed oil to name a few!

On the other hand, the Omega-6 Fatty Acid is responsible for many of the benefits mentioned above when consumed with Omega-3. The trick is to consume the right levels of these nutrients; you should be consuming double the amount of Omega-6 fatty acid as the Omega-3 or the benefits of these EFA's may actually be cancelled. The reason this is mentioned is because the world has become victim to fast food and frozen pre-made dishes, which actually have dangerously high amounts of Omega-6. However, following a whole foods based diet ensures your health as you'll get balanced amounts of each and every nutrient. Ultimately, Omega-6 can be found in seeds, nuts, green veggies, and oils, such as olive oil.

Lastly, the Omega-9 Fatty Acid is a non-essential fatty acid that the body can, in fact, produce. The body will produce this fatty acid only once there are appropriate levels of both Omega-3 and Omega-6, thus making it dependent on the consumption of the two fatty acids the body cannot produce. If you do not have appropriate amounts of Omega-3 and Omega-6 then you can in fact get additional Omega-9 from your diet (since your body wouldn't be producing it in this case). Omega-9 can be found naturally in plenty in avocados, nuts, chia seed oil and olive oil.

THE TRUTH ABOUT COCONUT OIL

As mentioned above, plant-based oils are great ketogenic vegan options containing unsaturated fats; however, coconut oil has received a more glorified view compared to the others. While coconut oil has a great, complementary flavor and can be used periodically, it has become overrated in the nutritional sense. While it has benefits such as decreasing bad cholesterol levels (LDL), these are only short term. Surprisingly, recent studies have uncovered that, in the long term, coconut oil can in fact negate health benefits by increasing the originally lowered LDL levels. So you can use coconut oil periodically as a majority of keto vegan recipes these days call for it; however, you can substitute as you wish with other plant based oils like hemp seed oil, flax seed oil, or olive oil to name a healthful few, as they not only lower LDL, but also increase HDL (good cholesterol).

Healthy Oils and Fats

Unsaturated fats decrease blood cholesterol when they replace saturated fats in the diet. You will find two types of unsaturated fat: monounsaturated fat and polyunsaturated fat. Monounsaturated fats have been shown to raise the level of HDL (the 'good' cholesterol that protects against heart attacks) within the blood, so in moderation they can be a component of a healthy diet. This is why they are referred to as the excellent fats. Olive, canola, and peanut oils are excellent sources of monounsaturated fats.

All fats, even the excellent ones, will still make you gain weight if too much is consumed. The key here is to maintain all fats in moderation but attempt to make the majority of your fat intake come from the good ones whenever possible. Note that a lot more than 20% of your daily calorie intake needs to be from fat of any kind, especially in the event you are attempting to lose weight.

WHAT IS KETO-VEGANISM

So now that we understand the concept of Keto and Veganism, let's dive into the brilliance of combining the two together. Both lifestyle choices are designed to help us help our bodies perform in the best way possible. Both are also about clean eating, however, applying the clean eating concepts of a ketogenic diet to the ethical eating view of veganism can torpedo your health and wellness substantially.

A vegan can also opt to take up a ketogenic vegan diet. A vegan is a person who prefers to eat plants such as potatoes, kale, plant products and beans. Some vegans also do not take honey. It is therefore evident that a vegan diet contains a high level of carbohydrates as a result of the sugar content and starch that is higher in plants than in animals. Having outlined this, a ketogenic vegan diet may appear to be impossible. However, it can be done.

A ketogenic vegan diet has to be obtained from plant foods that are particularly fatty, avoiding those that have high sugar or starch content. It is, however, a challenge as the access of fatty plants commercially is less than plants that are either sugary or starchy. This hinders the food selection. Therefore, the sole difference between a ketogenic diet and a vegan ketogenic diet is the strict consumption of plants in the latter. The end goal, however, is similar.

In the above chapters, we have explained both Vegan and Ketogenic diets individually. The focus of this chapter is going to be on a form of diet that came into existence by combining these two, i.e., Vegan and Ketogenic. It is called the Vegan Ketogenic Diet.

The Ketogenic diet lately has become the ultimate diet in terms of fat loss and ethical consumption, but meeting in the middle is never without compromise. The traditional Ketogenic diet is mainly based on consuming heavy animal fats. It would seem that the Ketogenic diet and Vegan diet are two opposite sides of a coin. This is because the Ketogenic diet promotes the consumption of mainly fats and some protein, while maintaining very low levels of carbohydrates, whereas a Vegan diet is an ideology based on the premise that all living creatures, including animals, should be respected, and that the killing and consumption of animals and animal-based ingredients breaches this premise. So, depending on the side you are on, we are sure that you would have ample reason to support your cause. But the question is, could these diets actually overlap? Is it possible to follow the principles of Veganism while enjoying the fat burning benefits of ketosis? The answer is YES! You can enjoy the best of both diets while still adhering to the ethical principles.

According to the conventional Keto rules, a person is only allowed to consume 20g of net carbs every day. However, for vegan following the ketogenic vegan diet, consuming 30g of net carbs is closer to achievable compared to the original 20g especially when no meat is involved, since all plant foods tend to have high carbohydrates as opposed to animal foods that are low in carbohydrates. So, consuming plant foods is going to increase the number of carbohydrates.

If you want to maintain the 20g carbs routine, we can assure you that all you would be eating, or we should say pouring, would be oil in your mouth all day. Besides being boring, this is also very unhealthy. We already said, to come in the middle there has to be a compromise. So you need to let go of the 20g carbs rule, and, by increasing just a small amount the target number of carbs, your food can be tasty and delicious. To maintain ketosis, it is recommended to not go over 30g, although there are many Vegan-Keto people who consume up to 50g of carbohydrates and still lose weight while maintaining a healthy, cruelty-free lifestyle. It is very dependent on the individual.

Below is the correct macronutrients ratio required for Keto diet
- *5-10 percent of calories should come from carbs.*
- *15-30 percent of calories should come from protein.*
- *60-75 percent of calories should come from fatty foods.*

On a vegan diet you focus on consuming plant-based foods, however, not all plant-based foods are equal in nutrient value for your body, nor are they equal in energy value for your body.

When applying the ketogenic philosophy to your vegan diet you can ensure that you are getting a stable level of green energy. The ketogenic lifestyle plan espouses the virtues of eating whole foods which help keep you energized and full. Ketogenic vegan foods ensure you are getting your nutrients without inundating your body with sugar.

We know that when you flood your body with sugar, you will get a short sugar high but then your energy levels will plummet. When your energy levels drop you get hungry again quickly and this could easily lead you to snack on quick snack foods that are high in fat and low on the nutrient scale. However, when you apply the ketogenic philosophy to the vegan diet you will ensure that you are only eating foods that are high in nutrients and energy without the influence of bad sugars.

GETTING ENOUGH LYSINE FROM A KETOGENIC VEGAN DIET

What is lysine?

Lysine is one of the nine amino acids our body cannot produce, as mentioned above. However, lysine is a necessary building block for our body as it plays extremely important roles in the development and creation of our protein. More importantly, lysine is mandatory for our growth, as well as converting fatty acids our body consumes into energy, which in turn keeps cholesterol levels at bay. Since lysine cannot be produced by our body, we must find it through the foods we eat on a daily basis.

The Importance of Lysine and How it Works

There are many uses of lysine. One of its interesting uses is in caramelization, which is applied to some desserts, like pastries. When it is heated, it links with fructose, glucose or any type of sugar to create a caramelized substance. Even though it offers many uses in the culinary field, the caramelized substance from lysine cannot be absorbed by the body. For that reason, all caramelized foods contain a low amount of lysine.

When inside the body, lysine is converted to acetyl CoA. It is an essential component in the metabolism of carbohydrates and in energy production.

It is the precursor to another amino acid known as carnitine, an amino acid required for transporting fatty acids into the mitochondria to produce energy and perform metabolic functions.

Lysine competes with arginine, which is another amino acid involved in the replication of the human simplex virus. In vitro studies, it was shown that arginine's growth-promoting action was inhibited by the presence of lysine. This is one of the reasons lysine is being given to treat and manage HSV outbreak.

Just like other essential amino acids, a deficiency of lysine may cause negative effects. These will include:

- Fatigue
- Nausea
- Dizziness
- Anorexia
- Slow growth
- Anemia

Why vegans sometimes don't get enough lysine

Lysine is an essential amino acid. This means that it cannot be synthesized by the body on its own. Therefore, it needs to come from dietary intake. Rich sources of this amino acid include animal proteins like meats and poultry. Milk is rich in this type of AA. But proteins from grains are low in lysine and wheat germ has high amounts of it. It is a generally known fact that foods containing the protein building block Lysine are found in flesh foods as well as dairy.

How much Lysine do you need and how can you get it?

Many sources say that adults should be consuming about 38-40mg per 1 kg of body weight of Lysine daily. Vegans can easily consume lysine in foods such as beans, nuts, lentils and all soy products. While it is essential to consume lysine in order for your body to have the appropriate nutrients it needs, there is a limit. Even though it can be pretty rare for keto vegans, too much Lysine can in fact be a bad thing. A spike in Lysine amino acids can cause an increase in cholesterol as well as stomach uneasiness and cramps.

Lysine rich protein vegan foods:

Remember that lysine is one of the nine vital amino acids that our body cannot produce. Moreover, it is commonly and mainly found in non-vegan foods including dairy, meat and, poultry, however, there are a few vegan options. Foods that contain high amounts of lysine include tempeh, lentils, black beans, quinoa, soy milk, pistachios and seitan.

NUTRIENT RICH VEGAN FOODS

Low carb ketogenic vegan foods

If you decide to embark on a ketogenic vegan diet, you'll really want to understand the nutritional value of nuts. They contain both protein and fat. They're tasty and some of nature's best nutrient sources. Essentially, they are foods with a lower carb amount than many other plant based foods.

Carbs in nuts & seeds

Nuts and seeds are easy to consume and very portable. They can be salty and oily making you yearn for them. Limit their consumption and do not eat those that are high in carbs like chestnuts, pistachios and cashews.

The serving size has been set to 1 ounce to make it easy to calculate a larger serving.

Food	Serving	Fats(g)	Carbs(g)	Fiber(g)	Protein(g)	Net Carbs(g)
Chai seed	1 oz.	9	12	11	4	1
Pecan	1 oz.	20	4	3	3	1
Flax Seed	1 oz.	12	8	7	5	1
Brazil Nut	1 oz.	19	4	2	4	2
Hazelnut	1 oz.	17	5	3	4	2
Walnut	1 oz.	18	4	2	4	2
Coconut, Unsweetened	1 oz.	18	7	5	2	2
Macadamia Nut	1 oz.	21	4	2	2	2

Food	Serving	Fats(g)	Carbs(g)	Fiber(g)	Protein(g)	Net Carbs(g)
Almond	1 oz.	15	5	3	6	2
Almond Flour	1 oz.	14	6	3	6	3
Pumpkin Seed	1 oz.	6	4	1	10	3
Sesame Seed	1 oz.	14	7	3	5	4
Sunflower Seed	1 oz.	14	7	3	6	4

Carbs in greens:

As we know, vegetables play an important role in a healthy, low-carb diet. You need to ensure that you choose the right kind of vegetables. Avoid those that have high sugars and do not make you lose weight. Choose the non-starchy options. Be careful when eating greens because some have a carb count that adds up at a rapid rate.

Food	Serving	Metric	Fats(g)	Carbs(g)	Fiber(g)	Protein(g)	Net Carbs(g)
Endive	2 oz.	56g	0	2	2	1	0
Butter head Lettuce	2 oz.	56g	0	1	0.5	1	0.5
Chicory	2 oz.	56g	0	2.5	2	1	0.5
Beet Greens	2 oz.	56g	0	2.5	2	1	0.5
Bok Choy	2 oz.	56g	0	1	0.5	1	0.5
Alfalfa Sprouts	2 oz.	56g	0	2	1	2	1
Spinach	2 oz.	56g	0	2	1	1.5	1
Swiss Chard	2 oz.	56g	0	2	1	1	1
Arugula	2 oz.	56g	0	2	1	1.5	1
Celery	2 oz.	56g	0	2	1	0.5	1
Chives	2 oz.	56g	0	2.5	1.5	2	1
Collard Greens	2 oz.	56g	0	3	2	1.5	1
Romaine lettuce	2 oz.	56g	0	2	1	1	1

Food	Serving	Metric	Fats(g)	Carbs(g)	Fiber(g)	Protein(g)	Net Carbs(g)
Asparagus	2 oz.	56g	0	2	1	1	1
Eggplant	2 oz.	56g	0	3	2	0.5	1
Radishes	2 oz.	56g	0	2	1	0.5	1
Tomatoes	2 oz.	56g	0	2	1	0.5	1
White mushrooms	2 oz.	56g	0	2	0.5	2	1.5
Cauliflower	2 oz.	56g	0	3	1.5	1	1.5
Cucumber	2 oz.	56g	0	2	0.5	0.5	1.5
Dill pickles	2 oz.	56g	0	2	0.5	0.5	1.5
Bell green pepper	2 oz.	56g	0	2.5	1	0.5	1.5
Cabbage	2 oz.	56g	0	3	1	1	2
Fennel	2 oz.	56g	0	4	2	1	2
Broccoli	2 oz.	56g	0	3.5	1.5	1.5	2
Green Beans	2 oz.	56g	0	4	2	1	2
Bamboo Shoots	2 oz.	56g	0	3	1	1.5	2

Carbs in fruits:

Fruit is the part of the plant that houses the seeds. Some fruits are known to be so because they are sweet. Other fruits include okra and green beans, among others. Avocado has a very low carb concentration compared to others.

Food	Serving	Metric	Fats(g)	Carbs(g)	Fiber(g)	Protein(g)	Net Carbs(g)
Rhubarb	2 oz.	56g	0	2.5	1	1	1.5
Lemon Juice	1 oz.	28g	0	2	0	0	2
Lime Juice	1 oz.	28g	0	2	0	0	2
Raspberries	2 oz.	56g	0	7	4	1	3
Blackberries	2 oz.	56g	0	6	3	1	3
Strawberries	2 oz.	56g	0	4	1	0	3

Protein rich vegan foods:

Proteins are commonly referred to as the building blocks of a person's life. Proteins are broken down into amino acids that are responsible for promoting the growth and repair of cells. They take longer to be digested compared to carbs. They make you remain fuller longer and have fewer calories. Some of the good vegetarian and vegan sources like tofu and lentils are outlined below.

Food	Serving	Metric	Fats(g)	Carbs(g)	Fiber(g)	Protein(g)	Net Carbs(g)
Tofu	100g	100g	9	4	2	16	2
Pumpkin seed	1 oz.	28g	6	4	1	10	3
Almond	1 oz.	28g	15	5	3	6	2
Flax Seed	1 oz.	28g	12	8	7	5	1
Chia Seed	1 oz.	28g	9	12	11	4	1
Brazil nut	1 oz.	28g	19	4	2	4	2
Hazelnut	1 oz.	28g	17	5	3	4	2
Walnut	1 oz.	28g	18	4	2	4	2
Pecan	1 oz.	28g	20	4	3	3	1
Unsweetened Coconut	1 oz.	28g	18	7	5	2	2
Macadamia nut	1 oz.	28g	21	4	2	2	2

Fat rich vegan foods:

It should be noted that our bodies need healthy fats like the monounsaturated and polyunsaturated fats. These fats have good levels of cholesterol and play a role in reducing diseases of the heart. Generally, fats from plant sources are very healthy. Avoid sources that have trans fats.

Food	Serving	Metric	Fats(g)	Carbs(g)	Fiber(g)	Protein(g)	Net Carbs(g)
Avocado oil	1 oz.	28g	28	0	0	0	0
Cocoa butter	1 oz.	28g	28	0	0	0	0
Coconut oil	1 oz.	28g	28	0	0	0	0
Flaxseed oil	1 oz.	28g	28	0	0	0	0
Macadamia oil	1 oz.	28g	28	0	0	0	0
MCT oil	1 oz.	28g	28	0	0	0	0
Olive oil	1 oz.	28g	28	0	0	0	0
Red palm oil	1 oz.	28g	28	0	0	0	0
Coconut cream	1 oz.	28g	10	2	1	1	1
Olives, green	1 oz.	28g	4	1	1	0	0
Avocado	1 oz.	28g	4	2	2	1	0

HOW TO COUNT CARBS?

Although most people on a low-carb diet count net carbs (total carbs minus fiber), the latest research hints at the importance of counting total carbs. In this scenario, consuming a very low-carb diet consisting of 20 grams or less of total carbs is the correct way to count carbs.

Although many believe that counting total carbs and ascribing to a very low-carb diet is the best way to lose weight, it is also important to understand how fiber works on blood sugar and, subsequently, overall metabolic health.

There are two types of fiber: soluble and insoluble. Most people think that dietary fiber does not affect blood sugar and that there are no calories given off at all, so they choose to use net carbs, total carbs minus fiber. However, this only applies to insoluble fiber, as this type of fiber cannot be absorbed by the body and doesn't affect blood sugar or ketosis.

Let's explain this in another way. Dietary fiber is indigestible and has two main components: insoluble fiber and soluble fiber. Once consumed, these fibers are fermented by the gut's microbiota into the short-chain fatty acid.

How does soluble fiber work?

The body absorbs calories from soluble fiber. The effect that it has on blood sugar is a bit more complicated. Ketosis can, in fact, be affected by soluble fiber because it is absorbed into the body and increases blood sugar, hence the discussion about using total carbs rather than net carbs.

When soluble fiber ferments in the large intestine, it starts producing gut hormones that help create a feeling of satiety. This appetite suppression is natural and contributes as the main reason that a low carb diet for weight loss can be very successful.

Recent studies have shown that soluble fiber plays a role in lowering blood sugar levels, although much more testing must be done to understand the effects of dietary fiber on metabolic health.

Total Carbs or Net Carbs?

High levels of ketones and low levels of glucose are not the main factors contributing to weight loss. Studies do not show that adding more ketones to the blood leads to greater and more rapid fat loss. In fact, the most important effect that a low-carb diet demonstrates, time and time again, is appetite suppression.

The body does not need to be in ketosis in order to lose weight. In fact, people who consume more than 50g of total carbs per day can continue to lose weight even though the body is not in any stage of ketosis.

There are differences of opinion whether to count total or net carbs regarding the "ideal" carb level. It has been suggested that ~ 50 grams of total carbs a day is enough to start nutritional ketosis. This is in between the range of 20-35 grams of net carbs depending on the fiber content. Most people on a ketogenic diet are successful in losing weight using this approach.

A different approach to a low carb diet recommends that you should have ~ 20 grams of total carbs a day. If you choose to track total carbs and follow a very low-carb diet, be sure to supplement your diet with necessary micronutrients, as extremely low-carb diets (20 grams of total carbs or less) are often deficient in several of these (magnesium, calcium, potassium, vitamin E, A, C, iron, thiamin, folate and zinc).

Above all, it is important to note that there is no wrong way to look at this. A ketogenic diet changes depending on what your goals are.

BALANCING MACRO-NUTRIENTS IN A KETOGENIC DIET

The challenge of a ketogenic vegan diet lies in getting a sufficient amount of calories, mainly from proteins and fats. You may calculate your daily calories or weight loss using various tools available to you at "http://happyhealthygreen. life/tools". As a rule of thumb, women are recommended to consume 2000 calories on a daily basis. For men, the amount is 2500.

A typical keto vegan diet, also known as a "long-chain triglyceride diet" usually includes a consumption ratio of 3 to 4 grams of fat for every 1 gram of carbohydrate and protein.

In order to ensure you are taking in accurate levels of each macro, you should make sure that you track your daily nutrient levels. The average percentage for each macro level for a ketogenic (vegan) diet is 5% carbohydrates, 20% protein, and 75% fats.

Macro	Protein	Carbs	Fat	Total Calories
Ratio	20%	5%	75%	
Calories	60	20	675	775
	120	40	1350	1510
	180	60	2025	2265
	240	80	2700	3020
	300	100	3375	3775

Important things to keep in mind

1. Always check your labels

Carbs are calculated differently depending on where you live. The U.S., Canada and other countries have labels where total carbs include fiber. So in order to calculate net carbs, you must deduct fiber from the total amount of carbs.

On the other hand, countries like the U.K. and Australia don't include fiber in the total carb amount labeled.

If you want to track total carbs for a very low-carb diet, be sure that your diet supplements you with the necessary micronutrients. Extremely low-carb diets (20 grams of total carbs or less) can often be deficient in several micronutrients (magnesium, calcium, potassium, vitamin E, A, C, iron, thiamin, folate and zinc).

2. Artificial Sweeteners

Most artificial sweeteners are often marketed as "sugar-free" or "zero carbs". Unfortunately, this isn't always the case. Some sweeteners like Stevia, Erythritol and Monk Fruit extract contain very few carbs while others like Xylitol or Tagatose contain massive amounts.

So, if you use products that contain Erythritol, Xylitol or sweeteners containing fructo-oligosaccharides (FOS), always remember to account for the added carbs.

3. Products Labeled "Low-carb"

Avoid most products labeled "low-carb" and "sugar free", etc. Most of these products contain more carbs than the manufacturer claims and are often processed with unhealthy ingredients.

LOSING WEIGHT WITH A KETOGENIC VEGAN DIET

Casual ketogenic diets (the kind people use for getting in shape, looking better and weight loss) are typically less than 50g-100g/day of carbs.

If you want to lose weight, a healthy weight-loss diet should not fall under 1700 calories daily for women and 2200 for men. A calorie count any lower than this would not be considered a responsible diet. With the recipes you'll find later in the book, you'll be able to calculate your daily calorie intake with respect to your personal goals. If you would like to speed up the weight loss process, you can always add an exercise or cardio routine to your daily and weekly schedules.

Obviously you can add your own nutrients and foods to the mix. In general, you should consume 30 to 100 grams of net carbs on a daily basis for your body to enter ketosis. Consuming a lesser amount of carbohydrates, and staying on the lower end of the scale at 30g per day, will ensure the body is in optimum ketosis and help you shed the weight right off.

According to various studies, the ketogenic diet for weight loss is characterized by the consumption of a maximum of 100g of carbs per day, representing around 5% of the calories consumed in the day. A typical diet usually provides between 45 and 65% of our calories in the form of carbohydrates. The remainder is distributed between lipids and proteins. In the ketogenic diet, the calories ingested in the form of lipids can reach up to 75%, and the proteins occupy the remaining 20%.

Usually, the body draws in the carbohydrates consumed each day for the energy needed for proper functioning of the body. In this diet, with carbohydrates being extremely limited, the body begins to tap into the carbohydrates that are stored in the muscles and liver called "glycogen" stores. As each gram of glycogen is bound to 3-4 g of water in the body, significant early weight loss in the ketogenic diet is actually a loss of water. When glycogen stores are depleted, the body begins to use lipids or fats to produce energy. When the body uses fat in the absence of carbohydrates, it produces waste products called ketones. Next, the ketone bodies begin to accumulate in the blood and their odor, similar to that of nail polish, becomes perceptible in the breath. This is the primary indicator that the body is in a "ketosis" state. It takes around 2 to 4 weeks before arriving at this condition. The state of "ketosis" can be checked by using ketone urine (acetoacetate) test strips such as Ketosis. All ketones are not used up when produced by the body. They will spill over into the urine and this is noted through the change of color in the urine strip.

This state of "ketosis" causes a marked decrease in appetite, which contributes to reducing the amount of food consumed. This condition can also lead to nausea and fatigue. Although the plan does not focus on counting calories, those who follow the diet absorb fewer calories because they do not get hungry, leading to weight loss.

According to many people, a few days after withdrawing from carbohydrates, they experienced increased energy levels. Why do you think this is the case? This is because a gram of fat has dense nutritional energy. Once you feel more energetic you can engage in different activities including working out to burn fat. In addition, once you start feeling much better, you are unlikely to succumb to emotional eating, which is the main culprit for many people who are overweight and obese.

The ketogenic diet also works because it is satiating. As mentioned earlier, a ketogenic diet is high in fat, adequate in protein and low in carbs. Fats are satiating and so are proteins. Thus, you will feel full longer and have no need to overeat.

The ketogenic diet also works because it helps activate fat metabolism due to the drastically reduced level of insulin in the body. Given that you reduce your intake of carbs, your blood has less glucose, meaning there won't be any need for the secretion of high amounts of insulin. Keep in mind that, besides facilitating the cells to absorb glucose, insulin has the effect of inhibiting fat metabolism (lipolysis). Instead, it actually promotes fat storage and glycogen accumulation (glycolysis). As such, with reduced insulin levels, your body can effectively start metabolizing fats since there is no inhibition.

Other factors that contribute to weight loss

Besides counting carbs, it's important to pay attention to how much protein and fat are consumed. It's a huge mistake to think that you can consume any amount of calories and still burn fat. If you eat too much, you will gain weight, even on a low-carb diet. To avoid that mistake, here are some very important principles to keep in mind.

- Be sure to eat enough protein, not just fat, because protein is the most sating macronutrient and helps combat cravings.

- Proper low-carb diets are naturally sating and act as appetite suppressants, which helps in the process of losing weight. In fact, you won't need to count calories all the time to lose weight and/or stay in ketosis.

- A mistake most people make is consuming far too many nuts, seeds and other fat bombs when trying to lose weight. You can hit a weight plateau or even gain weight simply because these are very calorie-dense per serving and thus exceed your caloric goals in order to lose weight.

- If there is no progress on your weight loss for more than 2-3 weeks, you should consider monitoring your calorie intake closely. There are several reasons why this could be happening. You might not be eating enough or you may be eating too much. As you get close to your ideal weight, losing weight generally gets harder.

- It is no problem to eat non-starchy vegetables such as cauliflower, spinach, kale, broccoli, zucchini and bell peppers, as well as fruits like avocados or berries. These fruits and vegetables pack a lot of micronutrients and are low in carbs so they won't impair your weight loss efforts at all and will, in fact, have a positive effect on overall metabolic health.

THE RELATIONSHIP BETWEEN EPILEPSY AND KETOGENIC DIET

Epilepsy is usually defined as a neurological condition as well as a group of neurological disorders. It has been observed to have long term effects in the life of the affected individual. The episodes of seizures characterize this condition and they are one of its main symptoms.

Symptoms of Epilepsy

Epilepsy is one of the more difficult neurologic conditions to diagnose. This is because of the multiple ways in which it can be caused. It is also because epilepsy can take on a wide variety of forms, manifesting unique symptoms on a case-by-case basis. Epileptic symptoms generally depend on which region of the brain is affected. Understanding the different signs and symptoms of this disease would go a long way in getting proper diagnosis, and ultimately proper treatment. The symptoms include:

- Seizures (generalized seizures and focal seizures)
- Stiffening of all muscles
- Loss of muscle control
- Presence of clonus, a condition where there's repeated rhythmic, jerking muscle movements
- Temporary loss of awareness
- Sensory disturbances, emotional swings, and spontaneous sensory disturbances

Some cases of epilepsy are caused by birth defects, brain tumors, stroke, or brain injury, but most cases of epilepsy have unknown etiologies.

It is estimated that 1% of people around the world have epilepsy. That amounts to around 65 million individuals. It should be noted that almost 80 percent of the cases of epilepsy are found in developing countries.

There are several treatment options available for people with epilepsy. One of them is brain surgery, which is one of the more frightening prospects that the general public faces. Medical experts say that years ago a surgeon would wait for years, even decades, before recommending surgery for epilepsy patients. However, surgical procedures have become better, safer, and more effective.

Specific diets have been developed to prevent seizures, with mixed results. Specific diet plans aim to reduce the incidences of epileptic attacks by manipulating how the brain works. This makes us arrive at another option of treatment which is the adoption of a ketogenic diet. Medical experts have achieved success at treating epileptic seizures using this diet. It's interesting that medical experts admit that it does work even though they do not know exactly how or why.

Since a ketogenic diet is a diet that features high fat, low carbohydrate, and controlled consumption of protein, it causes the body to use fat as the main source of energy. In many epileptic cases, switching to a ketogenic diet has resulted in a lowered incidence of seizures. However, the use of the ketogenic diet, especially for children, must be strictly monitored by trained medical specialists.

This diet has shown evidence that it can reduce the episodes of epileptic seizures in adults too when a less strict form of the diet is used. The results of current research studies suggest that the ketogenic diet protects neurons and modifies diseases for many adults who have neurodegenerative disorders. Some of the researches include '*A ketogenic diet as a potential novel therapeutic intervention in amyotrophic lateral sclerosis*' by Zhao et al, '*Ketogenic diet protects dopaminergic neurons against 6-OHDA neurotoxicity via up-regulating glutathione in a rat model of Parkinson's disease*' by Cheng et al and '*The ketogenic diet: metabolic influences on brain excitability and epilepsy*' by Lutas & Yellen. Still, the use of the diet to treat any form of epilepsy other than pediatric epilepsy is considered to be in the research stage.

A ketogenic diet allows patients to reduce the amount of anti-epileptic drugs they use as well as remain seizure-free. It is possible to stay seizure-free and completely stop depending on the drugs. This is highly beneficial to the patients since all medications administered as anti-seizure have side effects. The effects include reduced IQ, reduced concentration, and drowsiness as well as personality changes.

RECIPES

1. Flax Egg

Serves: 1
Prepping Time:
~1 min

Nutritional
Information
(per serving)

Calories: 37 kcal
Carbs: 2.1g
Fat: 2.7g
Protein: 1.1g
Fiber: 1.9g
Sugar: 0g

INGREDIENTS:

- 1 tablespoon ground flaxseed.
- 2 tablespoons spring water.

Total number of ingredients: 2

METHOD:

1. Mix flaxseed and spring water.
2. Allow to sit covered for 10 minutes.

Note: You can use this mixture to replace a single egg in any recipe.

TIP: *Many ketogenic recipes contain eggs; however, to be vegan-friendly, flax or chia eggs pose as great, low-carb alternatives.*

2. Almond Milk

INGREDIENTS:

- 1 cup raw almonds.
- 5 cups filtered water.
- 2 medjool dates, pitted.
- 1 teaspoon vanilla extract.
- 1 pinch sea salt.

Total number of ingredients: 5

METHOD:

1. Mix tap water with salt.
2. Place almonds in salt mixture.
3. Soak almonds overnight or for about 12 hours.
4. Remove almonds from salt mixture.
5. Rinse almonds in cold tap water.
6. Preheat oven to lowest setting.
7. Place rinsed almonds on a baking pan and put in oven to dry.
8. Once dry, remove almonds from oven and rinse again under cold water.
9. Add rinsed almonds to spring water.
10. Place mixture in a blender. Blend until creamy and smooth.
11. Strain mixture.
12. Place mixture back in blender.
13. Add vanilla and dates to mixture.
14. Blend until preferred milk consistency is reached.

Serves: 5
Prepping Time:
~60 min

Nutritional
Information
(per serving)

Calories: 191 kcal
Carbs: 12.8g
Fat: 13.2g
Protein: 5.4g
Fiber: 4.1g
Sugar: 7.6g

KETOGENIC
BREAD RECIPES

1. Banana Bread

Serves: 13
Prepping Time:
~5 min

Nutritional
Information
(per serving)

Calories: 106 kcal
Carbs: 12.1g
Fat: 17.9g
Protein: 5.3g
Fiber: 2.3g
Sugar: 5.2g

INGREDIENTS:

- 4 bananas.
- 4 flax eggs.
- 2 ½ cups almond flour.
- ⅓ cup olive oil.
- ½ tablespoon baking soda.

Total number of ingredients: 5

METHOD:

1. Preheat oven to 350 °F.
2. Slightly grease a loaf pan.
3. Chop bananas in quarter inch circular slices.
4. Place chopped bananas in a bowl.
5. Add flax eggs, almond flour, olive oil and baking soda to bowl.
6. Mix with spoon until well blended.
7. Pour mixture into loaf pan.
8. Bake for one hour.
9. Remove from oven and let cool at room temperature.

People on a ketogenic diet usually steer clear of eating bananas due to their high carb content (around 27g for an average sized banana). While this number seems scary, this recipe allows you to satisfy your banana sweet tooth while cutting the carb consumption per piece to about 12g.

2. Mini Italian Toast Crackers

Serves: 13
Prepping Time:
~5 min

Nutritional
Information
(per serving:
1 bun)

Calories: 225 kcal
Carbs: 5.4g
Fat: 20.9g
Protein: 6.2g
Fiber: 0.5g
Sugar: 1g

INGREDIENTS:

- 1 ¼ cups almond flour.
- 1 flax egg.
- 2 tablespoons olive oil.
- ¾ teaspoon salt.
- 1 ½ tablespoons Italian seasoning (or ¼ tsp. each of: basil, garlic powder, thyme, oregano and onion powder).

Total number of ingredients: 5

METHOD:

1. Preheat oven to 300 °F.
2. Place all ingredients into a bowl.
3. Mix ingredients into a dough-like consistency
4. Once dough is formed, place on a cutting board.
5. Shape dough into a thin, long, rectangular prism.
6. Using a knife, cut dough into thin pieces of your liking.
7. Lightly grease a baking tray.
8. Place cut dough on baking tray.
9. Bake for 10 minutes or until crisp.

These Italian crackers are sure to hit that savory spot with the Italian herbs adding a twist to your everyday cracker! Use these as crackers when you're craving a quick, crispy snack, or munch on them in the morning, spreading avocado on them to make a quick breakfast.

3. 2-Minute Microwave Burger Bun

Serves: 1
Prepping Time:
~3 min

Nutritional
Information
(per serving:
1 bun)

Calories: 280 kcal
Carbs: 10g
Fat: 23.9g
Protein: 9.5g
Fiber: 4.4g
Sugar: 1.4g

INGREDIENTS:

- ⅓ cup almond flour (or any other nut flour of your choice).
- 1 flax egg.
- ½ teaspoon baking powder.
- ½ teaspoon cocoa powder.
- ¼ teaspoon salt.
- ¾ teaspoon sesame seeds.

Total number of ingredients: 6

METHOD:

1. In a bowl add the almond flour, baking powder, cocoa powder and salt.
2. Mix thoroughly or you will end up tasting weird bits of baking powder, salt, or cocoa in your burger bun!
3. Add the flax egg to mixture and stir until well blended.
4. Slightly grease a cup large enough to fit the batter.
5. Sprinkle some of the sesame seeds at the bottom of the cup.
6. Pour batter on top of the seeds.
7. Sprinkle the rest of the seeds on top of the batter.
8. Place cup in microwave.
9. Microwave for about 2 minutes or until firm.

Sounds too easy to be true, right? Not to mention it makes the perfect complement to the perfect ketogenic vegan burger. This bun would be great with a seasoned tofu patty, grilled mushrooms and crisp, fresh veggies like tomato and lettuce.

4. Plain Loaf

Serves: 15
Prepping Time:
~10 min

———

Nutritional
Information
(per serving)

Calories: 90 kcal
Carbs: 1.5g
Fat: 9g
Protein: 0.5g
Fiber: 0.4g
Sugar: 0.4g

INGREDIENTS:

- ⅓ cup almond flour (or any other nut flour that you prefer).
- 3 flax eggs.
- ½ cup coconut or olive oil (either one works well depending on your taste preferences!).
- ¼ cup almond milk (or water, if you want to reduce the caloric content).
- 2 teaspoons baking powder.
- 1 teaspoon baking soda.
- ¼ teaspoon salt.

Total number of ingredients: 7

METHOD:

1. Preheat oven to 350 °F.
2. Lightly grease a loaf pan with oil.
3. Combine all ingredients, ensuring they are well combined.
4. Pour mixture into loaf pan and bake for about 1 hour.
5. Remove pan from oven and let loaf cool.
6. Once cooled, remove loaf by flipping pan upside down.
7. Slice evenly.

Note: Though this bread does not rise as much as a "normal" loaf would, per say, its plain taste is the perfect complement to a sandwich on the go! Also, if you decide to use this to make a quick, easy lunch, two slices yield only 3 grams of carbs for your daily count compared to a whopping 22 grams of your regular bread!

5. Italian Herb Rolls

Serves: 6
Prepping Time:
~10 min

___

Nutritional
Information
(per serving)

Calories: 257 kcal
Carbs: 16.6g
Fat: 18.6g
Protein: 5.8g
Fiber: 11.7g
Sugar: 1.5g

INGREDIENTS:

- 1 ¼ cups coconut flour.
- ¾ teaspoon baking soda.
- 6 tablespoons melted coconut oil.
- 3 tablespoons Italian seasoning (If you don't have this, you can just use 2/3 teaspoons each of: basil, garlic powder, thyme, oregano and onion powder).
- 3 flax eggs.
- ¾ teaspoon salt.

Total number of ingredients: 6

METHOD:

1. Preheat oven to 300 °F.
2. Add coconut flour, oil, baking soda and flax egg to a bowl.
3. Mix well.
4. Add Italian seasoning (or herbs if you don't have this seasoning) and salt to the mix.
5. Using your hands, mold the dough, small handfuls at a time, to make mini rolls. You should have about 6 rolls when done.
6. Place on a greased baking sheet.
7. Bake at 300 °F for about 45 minutes.
8. Remove from oven and cool at room temperature.

TIP: *The bread is naturally a bit crumbly, but if you don't let it cool for an extended period of time, it will completely fall apart.*

These lovely rolls are sure to satisfy cravings for carbs, and make a delectable side roll to any balanced meal, whether it be a salad, soup, or even as a snack with a drizzle of olive oil.

6. Tortilla Wraps

Serves: 6
Prepping Time:
~10 min

Nutritional
Information
(per serving)

Calories: 157 kcal
Carbs: 4.2g
Fat: 13.8g
Protein: 5.0g
Fiber: 1.9g
Sugar: 1.5g

INGREDIENTS:

- ¼ cup ground flaxseed.
- ¼ cup hot water.
- 1 cup almond flour.
- ¼ teaspoon baking powder.
- ½ teaspoon salt.

Total number of ingredients: 6

METHOD:

1. Mix ground flaxseed with hot water until you get a gel-like substance.
2. In a separate bowl, mix almond flour, salt and baking powder.
3. Add ground flaxseed mixture to almond flour mixture.
4. Mix thoroughly.
5. Add hot water as needed in order to achieve a perfect dough-like consistency.
6. Knead dough, then separate dough into about 6 balls.
7. Flatten each ball as thin as possible.
8. Grease a pan.
9. Place each tortilla on greased pan and bake each tortilla until brown on both sides.
10. Remove pan from oven.
11. Let cool completely before using as they are easier to mold and fold once cool.

This "bread based" recipe comes in handy if you're craving a good old tofu wrap or even a vegan-styled quesadilla!

TIP: *Psyllium husk and flaxseed mixed with hot water allows for a gel-like substance to form which is extremely convenient for achieving a dough type consistency.*

7. Keto-Vegan Pizza Crust

INGREDIENTS:

- 1 teaspoon salt.
- 1 tablespoon olive oil.
- 1 cup warm water.
- 2 ½ teaspoons active yeast.
- 3 cups almond flour.
- 1 pinch dried oregano, ground.
- 1 pinch dried basil, leaf.

Total number of ingredients: 7

METHOD:

1. Preheat oven to 300 °F.
2. Place warm water in a cup (Note: It must be the right temperature or else it will not work)
3. Add yeast to cup.
4. Stir for one minute until you see a light brown mixture
5. Let sit for 5 minutes until a thin layer of foam forms on top.
6. In a separate bowl, add almond flour and salt.
7. Mix almond flour and salt. Once done mixing, form a well in the middle of the almond flour-salt mixture.
8. Pour yeast mixture and olive oil into well center and begin mixing ingredients.
9. Mix well until a dough is achieved. Add more or less flour depending on consistency of dough.
10. Separate into 2 balls.
11. Using a rolling pin, flatten balls into circles of dough.
12. Place dough in oven and allow to cook halfway.
13. Take out dough.
14. Place pizza toppings on dough.
15. Place pizza dough back in oven to finish baking.
16. Once baked, remove from oven.
17. Let cool for 2 minutes, then use a pizza slicer to slice into 8 pieces per pizza.

This adapted ketogenic vegan pizza crust is the perfect substitute if you're looking for a quick pizza without the excess carbs. This crust works best as thin to regular crust, but not deep dish. Pair with some fresh tomato sauce, vegan cashew-parmesan cheese, mushrooms, spinach and even tofu if you like!

Serves: 2
Prepping Time:
~10 min

Nutritional Information (per serving: 1 Crust Slice)

Calories: 134 kcal
Carbs: 3.4g
Fat: 11.8g
Protein: 4.9g
Fiber: 6.3g
Sugar: 1.6g

8. Panini Flat Bread

Serves: 10
Prepping Time:
~10 min

Nutritional
Information
(per serving:
2 half slices/
one sandwich)

Calories: 280 kcal
Carbs: 8.1g
Fat: 24.4g
Protein: 8.5g
Fiber: 3.7g
Sugar: 3.1g

INGREDIENTS:

- 3 cups almond flour.
- 4 flax eggs.
- ⅓ cup coconut flour.
- 1 teaspoon baking soda.
- ½ teaspoon garlic powder.
- ¼ cup water.
- ¼ cup olive oil.

Total number of ingredients: 7

METHOD:

1. Preheat oven to 350 °F.
2. Mix dry ingredients (coconut flour, almond flour, garlic powder and baking soda) together in a bowl.
3. To this bowl, add in flax eggs, olive oil and water and mix completely until a dough forms (add extra flour or water accordingly, it should be a bit sticky!).
4. Place dough onto a parchment paper-covered tray and mold into a rough rectangular loaf shape.
5. Place 1 piece of parchment paper on top of loaf.
6. Place loaf in oven and bake for 15-20 minutes until firm.
7. Remove loaf from oven.
8. Remove top piece of parchment paper and let loaf cool completely.
9. Once cool, cut into about 10 square pieces, then cut each piece in half.

This bread is great if you're craving a sandwich with a twist! Have a pressed spinach and Portobello mushroom sandwich with just a small handful of vegan cashew cheese to indulge.

The bonus in this recipe is the added protein powder and almond flour. You are able to get a dough-like consistency with minimal carbs and a great dose of protein at 8.5g per sandwich.

9. Herb Cracker Crisps

Serves: 20
Prepping Time:
~5 min

___

Nutritional
Information
(per serving:
about 4 crackers)

Calories: 201 kcal
Carbs: 4.7g
Fat: 18.4g
Protein: 5.5g
Fiber: 0.4g
Sugar: 1.8g

INGREDIENTS:

- 1 cup almond flour.
- 2 flax eggs.
- 2 tablespoons canola oil.
- 2 tablespoons water.
- 1 tablespoon rosemary (can be fresh or dried, but freshly chopped rosemary is preferable as it will give a beautiful, strong taste!).
- ½ teaspoon garlic powder.
- ¼ teaspoon dried oregano, ground.
- ¼ teaspoon dried basil, leaf.
- ¼ teaspoon salt.
- 1 pinch black pepper.

Total number of ingredients: 10

METHOD:

1. Preheat oven to 350 °F.
2. Place all ingredients in a bowl and mix well.
3. Line a pan with non-stick parchment paper.
4. Taking the dough formed in step 2, scoop ½ tablespoon of dough and place on pan. Flatten with your finger to make it cracker-width.
5. Bake for about 5-10 minutes until the outsides are crisp and the insides are just the slightest bit soft (they'll harden even more when cooling).
6. Remove from oven and let cool.

Eat these lovely crisps alone or with a spread to please any cracker-snack cravings you may be having. The infusion of herbs is sure to hit your taste buds and leave you satisfied, with only 4.7g of carbs and 1.8g of sugar per serving!

10. Dried Fruits and Nuts Breakfast Bread

Serves: 15
Prepping Time:
~15 min

Nutritional
Information
(per serving)

Calories: 315 kcal
Carbs: 21.1g
Fat: 19.4g
Protein: 6.1g
Fiber: 3.6g
Sugar: 15.1g

INGREDIENTS:

- 2 cups almond flour.
- 1 medium banana.
- 2 flax eggs.
- ¼ cup coconut oil.
- 2 tablespoons whole flax seeds.
- ¼ teaspoon salt.
- ½ teaspoon baking soda.
- 1 ½ cups roughly chopped dried mixed fruit (e.g., cranberries, strawberries, pineapple, cherries).
- 1 ½ cups roughly chopped dried nuts (e.g., pecans, almonds, walnuts).

Total number of ingredients: 10

METHOD:

1. Preheat oven to 300 °F.
2. Lightly grease a loaf pan with olive oil.
3. Place bananas in a bowl and mash extremely well.
4. To the mashed bananas, add coconut oil and flax eggs.
5. Mix well.
6. To the mixture, add in flour, baking powder and salt and mix thoroughly.
7. Top with fruits, nuts and seeds and mix until everything is evenly mixed.
8. Pour batter in greased loaf pan and let bake for about 45 minutes or until knife comes out of the center clean.
9. Remove pan from oven and let cool completely before slicing.

*This bread does not rise, so no worries if you don't see that happening!

You will realize how many nutrients you are getting when you eat a slice, as well as how satisfied and strengthened you will feel! Due to the amount of dried fruits and nuts in the recipe, as well as the density of the loaf, one to two slices is more than enough to get you energized and full until lunch time. You can even grab a slice if you're looking for a boost in between your meals.

The great thing about this recipe is that it is very adaptable. You can choose whatever assortments of dried fruits or nuts you want to add to the recipe.

11. Seed and Nut Topped Loaf

Serves: 15
Prepping Time:
~15 min

Nutritional
Information
(per serving)

Calories: 172 kcal
Carbs: 8.1g
Fat: 13.2g
Protein: 6.1g
Fiber: 3.5g
Sugar: 2.4

INGREDIENTS:

- 2 cups almond flour.
- 2 tablespoons coconut flour.
- ½ cup whole almonds.
- 3 tablespoons sesame seeds.
- ½ cup pumpkin seeds.
- ¼ cup whole flax seeds.
- ½ teaspoon salt.
- 3 flax eggs.
- 1 ½ teaspoons baking soda.
- ¾ cup almond milk.
- 3 drops stevia sweetener.
- 1 tablespoon apple cider vinegar.

Total number of ingredients: 12

METHOD:

1. Preheat oven to 350 °F.
2. Blend almonds in a blender until fine.
3. Add flax seeds, sesame seeds and pumpkin seeds and blend.
4. Add almond flour, coconut flour, salt and baking soda and blend.
5. In a separate bowl, add flax eggs, coconut oil, almond milk, vinegar and sweetener and stir well.
6. Add almond mixture to flax egg mixture and let sit for a few minutes.
7. Grease a loaf pan.
8. Pour batter in pan.
9. Sprinkle left over seeds atop batter (pumpkin, flax, and sesame seeds).
10. Bake for about 45 minutes or until a knife comes clean out of the middle.
11. Remove from oven and let cool completely before slicing.

This loaf recipe is a dry, nutty spin on a regular bread loaf. What makes it even better is its low carb, high fat content, allowing you to consume a few pieces guilt free.

12. Low Carb Corn Bread

Serves: 18
Prepping Time:
~10 min

Nutritional
Information
(per serving)

Calories: 138 kcal
Carbs: 7.2g
Fat: 10.7g
Protein: 3.5g
Fiber: 1.2g
Sugar: 2.6g

INGREDIENTS:

- 2 cups almond flour.
- 6 drops stevia sweetener.
- 1 teaspoon salt.
- 2 flax eggs.
- 3 ½ teaspoons baking powder.
- ½ cup vanilla flavored almond milk.
- ⅓ cup coconut oil.
- 15 oz. can baby corn, finely chopped.

Total number of ingredients: 8

METHOD:

1. Preheat oven to 350 °F.
2. In a bowl, mix almond flour, salt and baking powder.
3. Add stevia, chopped corn, flax eggs, almond milk and coconut oil.
4. Mix well, ensuring no clumps.
5. Lightly grease a pan.
6. Pour batter in pan.
7. Place pan in oven and let bake 50-60 minutes or until knife comes cleanly out of the middle.

You would think that people on a ketogenic diet would need to steer clear of corn, but here's a recipe that has been tweaked to prove otherwise! The stevia acts as a natural sweetener with almond meal acting as a substitute for high carb flour options. You can eat a slice for breakfast or in between meals to satisfy cravings.

13. Low Carb Sub Bread

Serves: 4 mini subs
Prepping Time:
~5 min

Nutritional
Information
(per serving)

Calories: 292 kcal
Carbs: 13.3g
Fat: 23.2g
Protein: 9.9g
Fiber 2,5g
Sugar: 3.2g

INGREDIENTS:

- 1 ½ cups almond flour.
- 5 tablespoons psyllium husk powder, finely ground.
- 2 teaspoons baking powder.
- 1 teaspoon salt.
- 2 ½ tablespoons apple cider vinegar.
- 2 flax eggs.
- 1 cup boiling water.

Total number of ingredients: 7

METHOD:

1. Preheat oven to 350 °F.
2. In a bowl, mix together almond flour, psyllium husk powder, baking powder and salt.
3. Add flax eggs and apple cider vinegar and mix well until a dough forms.
4. Add boiling water and continue mixing.
5. Mold dough into 4 mini subs or one large sub (remember the dough should and will rise).
6. Place dough on a slightly greased baking pan and let bake for 45 minutes or until firm.

Yes, while 13.3g carbs may seem like a lot, it must be taken in comparison to a traditional sub sandwich's carb levels: a whole 40g. Enjoy this recipe when you find yourself reminiscing on those tasty sub sandwiches, and simply indulge the guilt-free way!

14. Plain Loaf

Serves: 15
Prepping Time:
~5 min

**Nutritional
Information
(per serving)**

Calories: 142 kcal
Carbs: 5.4g
Fat: 11.8g
Protein: 3.9g
Fiber: 3,5g
Sugar: 1.5g

INGREDIENTS:

- ½ cup coconut flour.
- 1 ½ cups almond flour.
- ¼ cup flax seed.
- 5 flax eggs.
- 4 tablespoons coconut oil (melted).
- ½ teaspoon baking powder.
- ¼ teaspoon salt.
- 1 tablespoon apple cider vinegar.

Total number of ingredients: 8

METHOD:

1. Preheat oven to 350 °F.
2. In a bowl, mix together dry ingredients: almond flour, coconut flour, baking powder, salt and flax seeds.
3. In a separate bowl mix together coconut oil and apple cider vinegar.
4. Combine dry and liquid ingredients from Steps 2 and 3. Mix well.
5. Pour batter in a slightly greased loaf pan.
6. Bake for 30-45 minutes or until firm.
7. NOTE: Make sure the loaf is completely cooled before slicing it.

Here is another spin on a plain bread type loaf that you could use a spread on, or for on-the-go sandwiches!

15. Seed-Based Crackers

Serves: 25 crackers
Prepping Time:
~5 min

___

Nutritional
Information
(per serving)

Calories: 53 kcal
Carbs: 3.5g
Fat: 3.6g
Protein: 1.6g
Fiber: 1.6g
Sugar: 0.1g

INGREDIENTS:

- 1 cup flaxseed, ground.
- 1 cup pumpkin seeds.
- ½ cup sesame seeds.
- ½ teaspoon salt.
- 1 cup hot water.

Total number of ingredients: 5

METHOD:

1. Preheat oven to 300 °F.
2. Place all ingredients in a bowl and mix.
3. Let sit 5 minutes (The flaxseed will form a gel with the water).
4. Spread mixture on a parchment paper-lined pan.
5. Using a knife, cut dough evenly into about 25 crackers.
6. Place in oven and bake till firm.
7. Turn oven off, leaving crackers in oven for about 1 hour so that crackers dry out.

Simple and quick homemade crackers are sure to satisfy your need of a quick snack, or even to use as a base to throw a low carb spread on.

16. 2-Minute Microwave Fruit Bread in a Mug!

Serves: 4 slices
Prepping Time:
~3 min

Nutritional
Information
(per serving:
1 circled slice)

Calories: 165 kcal
Carbs: 25.5g
Fat: 6.2g
Protein: 4.1g
Fiber: 0.8g
Sugar: 13.3g

INGREDIENTS:

- ⅓ cup almond flour (or any other nut flour of your preference).
- 1 flax egg.
- ¼ teaspoon baking soda.
- ¼ teaspoon salt.
- 2 tablespoons of your desired dried fruit (For this recipe, raspberries and strawberries were chosen).

Total number of ingredients: 5

METHOD:

1. To a bowl, add almond flour, baking soda, dried fruits and salt. Mix thoroughly.
2. Add flax egg and stir until evenly distributed. Also make sure dried fruits are evenly distributed in the batter.
3. Lightly grease a mug that is big enough to fit batter.
4. Pour batter into mug and microwave for about 2 minutes.
5. Remove mug from oven and slice mini loaf into about 4 pieces.

This recipe is an adaptation of the new craze of "microwave bread" which allows you to exhaust minimal effort yet indulge to the maximum.

Raspberries and Strawberries are great for those on a ketogenic diet as fresh raspberries contain 3.3g of carbs per ounce and strawberries 2.2g. Ultimately, this recipe is such an efficient, tasty, and filling way to put a spin on your normal loaf of bread.

17. Chunky Almond Coconut Bread

Serves: 10
Prepping Time:
~8 min

Nutritional
Information
(per serving)

Calories: 199 kcal
Carbs: 6.2g
Fat: 17.4g
Protein: 5.3g
Fiber: 3.2g
Sugar: 1.8g

INGREDIENTS:

- 1 ½ cups almond flour.
- 2 tablespoons coconut flour.
- ¼ cup flaxseed, ground.
- ¼ teaspoon salt.
- 5 flax eggs.
- 1 ½ teaspoons baking soda.
- 3 drops stevia sweetener.
- ¼ cup coconut oil.
- 1 tablespoon apple cider vinegar.
- 1 tablespoon almonds, chopped.

Total number of ingredients: 10

METHOD:

1. Preheat oven to 350 °F.
2. Mix all dry ingredients: almond flour, coconut flour, salt, flax and baking soda in a blender.
3. Add in stevia, flax eggs, apple cider vinegar and coconut oil.
4. Blend extremely well making sure there are no clumps.
5. Remove batter from blender and place in a bowl.
6. Add chopped almonds and mix to ensure almonds are evenly distributed.
7. Place batter in a lightly greased loaf pan and bake for 30-35 minutes.

This energy booster is sure to meet your dietary and taste bud needs. With the extra handful of almond chunks, you will be satiated and strengthened!

VEGAN FAT BOMBS

1. Coconut Berry Bombs

Serves: 16 cubes
Prepping Time:
~5 min

___

Nutritional
Information
(per serving)

Calories: 217 kcal
Carbs: 4.0g
Fat: 21.9g
Protein: 1.1g
Fiber: 2.2g
Sugar: 1.5g

INGREDIENTS:

- 1 cup coconut butter.
- 1 cup coconut oil.
- ½ cup fresh or frozen fruit of your choice (raspberries, blackberries, blueberries, etc.).
- ½ teaspoon sweetener of your choice (for example: 3 drops of stevia).
- ¼ teaspoon vanilla powder.
- 1 tablespoon lemon juice.

Total number of ingredients: 6

METHOD:

1. Place coconut oil, coconut butter and fruit (only if you chose frozen fruit) in a pot and heat on stove.
2. Mix thoroughly, then let cool.
3. Place mixture in a blender.
4. Add remaining ingredients to blender.
5. Blend until smooth.
6. Spread mix on a pan lined with parchment paper. Spread evenly.
7. Place in refrigerator for about an hour or until cold and firm.
8. Once cold, cut into about 16 squares and put back into refrigerator.

For starters, this is a great recipe as it contains 21.9g of plant based fats and only 4g of carbs per cube - wow! Moreover, this recipe is extremely versatile to cater to a plethora of taste buds. Just follow the directions above, adding whatever fruit you prefer!

2. Oats and Fudge Squares

INGREDIENTS:

- 1 cup coconut oil, melted (or melted oil of your choice).
- ½ cup shredded coconut, unsweetened.
- ⅓ cup coconut flour.
- ½ teaspoon vanilla extract.
- 2 cups hemp hearts.

For the Fudge Middle:
- 10 oz. 100% dark chocolate.
- ½ cup coconut milk.

Total number of ingredients: 7

METHOD:

1. Melt chocolate and coconut milk in a saucepan and stir until smooth.
2. Mix melted coconut oil, shredded coconut, coconut flour, vanilla extract and hemp hearts in heated saucepan. Mix well, then remove from heat.
3. Press half of shredded coconut mixture onto a lightly greased pan, then alternate and add the chocolate filling, layering evenly. Then place the other half of shredded coconut mixture on top and press gently.
4. Refrigerate overnight, then cut into squares.

Vegans try to avoid grains and oats, so behold the oats 'n' fudge recipe! They taste just like real oats, but without the carbs, and with plenty of fat. The secret to this recipe is the hemp hearts with 13.5g of fat per 3 tablespoons and only 2g of carbs, so be sure to have some on hand!

Serves: 16 cubes
Prepping Time:
~20 min

Nutritional
Information
(per serving)

Calories: 300 kcal
Carbs: 5.0g
Fat: 28g
Protein: 8g
Fiber: 4g
Sugar: 1.5g

3. Mini Choco-Coco Cups

Serves: 16 cups
Prepping Time:
~35 min

___

Nutritional
Information
(per serving)

Calories: 39 kcal
Carbs: 7.9g
Fat: 3.7g
Protein: 5.8g
Fiber: 5.5g
Sugar: 1.4g

INGREDIENTS:

For the coconut based bottom:
- ½ cup coconut butter.
- ½ cup coconut oil.
- ½ cup unsweetened coconut, shredded.
- 1 tablespoon vanilla extract.
- 12 drops of stevia.

For the chocolate based top:
- Sugar-free, milk free, 100% dark chocolate (If you prefer to make homemade chocolate sauce it will work for this recipe as well!).

Total number of ingredients: 6

METHOD:

1. Line a mini muffin pan with mini cupcake liners
2. Place coconut butter and coconut oil in a heated pan and melt at low heat, stirring constantly.
3. Add shredded coconut and vanilla.
4. Pour mixture into cupcake liners and let sit in freezer for 30 minutes until firm.
5. Melt chocolate and scoop it over hardened coconut candies.
6. Place candies in refrigerator and keep refrigerated until candy is firm.

These lovely bites will remind you of mini Reese's Cups but with a twist! For those of you with a coconut sweet tooth, this combination paired with the chocolate on top is great for satisfying your cravings and giving you a quick energy boost.

4. Nut Mania Fat Bomb

Serves: 36
Prepping Time:
~15 min

Nutritional
Information
(per serving)

Calories: 217 kcal
Carbs: 3.4g
Fat: 21.7g
Protein: 0.4g
Fiber: 1.7g
Sugar: 0.6g

INGREDIENTS:

- ½ cup cocoa butter.
- 1 cup almond butter.
- 1 cup coconut butter.
- 1 cup coconut oil.
- ½ cup coconut milk.
- ¼ cup olive oil.
- 1 tablespoon vanilla extract.
- ¼ cup chopped almonds.
- ¼ teaspoon salt.
- ¼ cup shelled pistachios, roasted.

Total number of ingredients: 10

METHOD:

1. Melt cocoa butter over low heat, stirring frequently.
2. Add all other ingredients (except the almonds) to an electric mixing bowl and mix thoroughly.
3. Stir in melted cocoa butter and mix again.
4. Spread mixture on a parchment lined pan.
5. Place chopped almonds on top.
6. Refrigerate overnight.

What better way to get satiated and get an energy boost from a quick bite than from a yummy nut-based treat?! This recipe is versatile as you can use whatever nuts you desire. Pistachios and almonds work best. Grab a few on the go to keep you full throughout the day.

5. Coconut Balls

Serves: 18
Prepping Time:
~5 min

Nutritional
Information
(per serving)

Calories: 143 kcal
Carbs: 1.5g
Fat: 14.9g
Protein: 0.5g
Fiber: 0.8g
Sugar: 0.3g

INGREDIENTS:

- 1 cup coconut oil (softened, not melted).
- 1 teaspoon vanilla extract.
- 5 drops of stevia.
- 1 teaspoon salt.
- 3 tablespoons 100% cocoa powder.
- 2 tablespoons almond butter (or whatever nut butter you prefer).
- ½ cup unsweetened coconut, shredded.

Total number of ingredients: 7

METHOD:

1. Mix all the ingredients together (make sure there are no clumps or uneven areas).
2. Take small ball-shaped tablespoons of dough and roll them in shredded coconut.
3. Place finished bites on a pan lined with parchment paper and refrigerate until solid.

Many of these recipes opt for using coconut based ingredients as they are high in fat and low on the carbohydrate scale. So for those of you coconut lovers, you're in luck. If not, no worries, as there's an array of different flavored fat bombs coming up!

6. Lemon Zest Fat Bombs

Serves: 16 cubes
Prepping Time:
~10 min

Nutritional
Information
(per serving)

Calories: 78 kcal
Carbs: 1.7g
Fat: 7.7g
Protein: 0.5g
Fiber: 1.1g
Sugar: 0.5g

INGREDIENTS:

- ½ cup coconut butter (also sold in stores as creamed coconut, NOT coconut milk).
- ¼ cup coconut oil, softened.
- lemon zest, finely grated from 1-2 lemons.
- 3 drops of stevia.
- 1 pinch of salt.

Total number of ingredients: 5

METHOD:

1. Mix together all the ingredients, ensuring even mixing.
2. Fill each mini cupcake mold with 1 tablespoon of the mixture.
3. Place tray in fridge for about an hour or until firm.

Here's a spin on the coconut chocolate cups mentioned above for those of you into that lemony flavor. This is a guilt-free indulgence with 7.7g of fat and only 1.7g of carbs, not to mention less than 1g of sugar, yet you still taste the lemony, sweet combination!

7. Strawberry Coconut Fat Bombs

Serves: 15
Prepping Time:
~10 min

Nutritional
Information
(per serving)

Calories: 81 kcal
Carbs: 1.6g
Fat: 8.1g
Protein: 0.4g
Fiber: 1g
Sugar: 0.6g

INGREDIENTS:

- ⅓ cup coconut butter.
- ⅓ cup coconut oil.
- ½ tablespoon 100% cocoa powder.
- 2 drops stevia sweetener (or whatever natural sweetener you personally prefer).
- ⅓ cup fresh strawberries.
- 1 tablespoon shredded coconut, unsweetened.

Total number of ingredients: 6

METHOD:

1. To a pot, add coconut butter, coconut oil, syrup and cocoa powder.
2. Cook over low heat until melted, stirring constantly.
3. To a frying pan, add strawberries with a bit of water and crush them down, stirring constantly.
4. Place strawberries in a blender, along with one tablespoon of the coconut oil mixture, and blend.
5. Fill each mold of your choice with coconut oil mixture and one tablespoon each of strawberry mixture.
6. Sprinkle shredded coconut on top of each mold.
7. Place in refrigerator and refrigerate overnight.

The combination of strawberries and coconut is delicious, even if you're skeptical at first; everyone should give it a try! This recipe's ingredients are very adaptable as you can substitute so many ingredients to fix the nutritional values to your dietary needs. You can change the preference of fruit, sweetener, and even oils and butters used to nut-based ones if you prefer!

8. Walnut Chocolate Bars

Serves: 15
Prepping Time:
~10 min

___

Nutritional
Information
(per serving)

Calories: 691 kcal
Carbs: 14.4g
Fat: 64.7g
Protein: 12.8g
Fiber: 0.5g
Sugar: 3.3g

INGREDIENTS:

- ½ cup coconut oil (melted).
- 4 tablespoons cocoa powder.
- 1 tablespoon sugar (or sweetener of your choice).
- 2 tablespoons tahini paste.
- ¼ cup halved walnuts.

Total number of ingredients: 5

METHOD:

1. Place all the ingredients except the walnuts in a pot on low heat.
2. Stir constantly until melted.
3. Let cool.
4. Pour mixture into molds (or ice trays) and place in refrigerator.
5. Once bars are almost firm, add a halved walnut on top of each bar and continue to refrigerate.

While we are trying to decrease our sugars, it seems that sugar works best in this recipe. 1 tablespoon has 12g of sugar, but this is for 15 bars. If you have a go-to natural sweetener that you find better, by all means use it!

9. Maple Pecan Fat Bombs

INGREDIENTS:

- 2 cups pecan halves.
- 1 cup almond flour.
- ½ cup shredded coconut, unsweetened.
- ½ cup coconut oil.
- ¼ teaspoon stevia sweetener or maple syrup.

Total number of ingredients: 5

METHOD:

1. Preheat oven to 350 °F.
2. Place pecans on a parchment-lined tray and place in oven.
3. Toast pecans for 5 minutes.
4. Remove pecans from oven and place on a cutting board.
5. Using a rolling pin, crush the pecans.
6. Place dry ingredients in a bowl and mix evenly.
7. Add wet ingredients and mix evenly. A crumbly-type dough will form.
8. Place dough on a parchment-lined pan and bake for 25 minutes.
9. Remove from oven and let cool at room temperature.
10. Once cooled, place in refrigerator.

While this fat bomb does take a bit more time, it's an amazing grab 'n' go on the way out to work, or in the evening before you sleep. Each bar contains fat levels of 28g with about 5g of carbs. And, like most recipes, if pecans are not your preference, you can substitute with another nut of your choice.

Serves: 12
Prepping Time:
~15 min

Nutritional
Information
(per serving)

Calories: 285 kcal
Carbs: 5.1g
Fat: 28g
Protein: 3.7g
Fiber: 2.8g
Sugar: 1.8g

10. Peanut Butter Pecan Bars

Serves: 4
Prepping Time:
~15 min

___

Nutritional
Information
(per serving)

Calories: 678 kcal
Carbs: 14.2g
Fat: 64.4g
Protein: 9.8g
Fiber: 2g
Sugar: 7.5g

INGREDIENTS:

- ½ cup peanut butter.
- ½ cup coconut oil.
- 1 teaspoon vanilla extract.
- 1 tablespoon vanilla syrup.
- 1 cup pecans.

Total number of ingredients: 5

METHOD:

1. Place coconut oil and peanut butter in a bowl and mix.
2. Warm mixture in a microwave for 30 seconds, then take out and mix some more.
3. Place mixture back in microwave for another 30 seconds. Repeat process until mixture is smooth.
4. Add extract, syrup and pecans and stir until well blended.
5. Separate mix into 4 separate rectangular molds to give thin, rectangular bar shape.
6. Place bars in refrigerator and let cool until firm.

11. Dark Chocolate Almond Clusters

Serves: 10
Prepping Time:
~15 min

___

Nutritional
Information
(per serving)

Calories: 249 kcal
Carbs: 6.1g
Fat: 22.1g
Protein: 7.2g
Fiber: 4.3g
Sugar: 0.7g

INGREDIENTS:

- 1 cup almonds.
- ⅓ teaspoon stevia.
- 10 oz. store bought dairy free, sugar free dark chocolate.

Total number of ingredients: 3

METHOD:

1. Mix almonds with sweetener and separate into 8 clusters (the sticky sweetener should allow almonds to stick together).
2. Melt chocolate in a pot on low heat and let cool.
3. Dip each almond cluster into chocolate sauce and place on a tray lined with parchment paper.
4. Place tray in freezer for 30 minutes, then refrigerate.

Having chocolate cravings? This recipe has you covered. Again, if you prefer homemade chocolate sauce, this recipe will work just as well. It also works just as well if you substitute the stevia with another natural sweetener you're more accustomed to!

12. Raspberry Almond Chocolate Brittle

Serves: 8
Prepping Time:
~5 min

Nutritional
Information
(per serving)

Calories: 148 kcal
Carbs: 6.5g
Fat: 12.5g
Protein: 2.7g
Fiber: 2.1g
Sugar: 2.4g

INGREDIENTS:

- ¼ cup almond butter.
- ¼ cup coconut butter.
- 1 tablespoon cocoa powder.
- ¼ cup raw almonds, chopped.
- ¼ cup walnuts, chopped.
- ¼ cup frozen raspberries.

Total number of ingredients: 6

METHOD:

1. Place coconut butter, cocoa powder and almond butter in a bowl and mix.
2. Microwave raspberries for 45 seconds.
3. On a non-stick pan, pour butter mixture and top with chopped nuts and melted raspberries.
4. Place tray in freezer for an hour, or until frozen, then break into about 8 pieces.

The combination of fruits, nuts, and chocolate will make this your favorite go-to fat bomb for at least a while! While it doesn't have as much fat as the other recipes, it can do the trick for those of you looking for some tasty, quick energy.

13. Chocolate Orange Nut Clusters

Serves: 25
Prepping Time:
~5 min

Nutritional
Information
(per serving)

Calories: 66 kcal
Carbs: 1.5g
Fat: 9.3g
Protein: 1.1g
Fiber: 0,9g
Sugar: 0.2g

INGREDIENTS:

- ½ cup pure dark cocoa powder.
- ¼ cup coconut oil.
- 1 ⅓ cups walnuts, chopped (or any nut of your preference).
- 1 teaspoon cinnamon.
- ½ tablespoon orange zest (finely grated).

Total number of ingredients: 5

METHOD:

1. Place dark chocolate along with a bit of water in a pot.
2. Stir on low heat.
3. Add coconut oil, orange zest, chopped walnuts and cinnamon and stir well.
4. Spoon about one tablespoon each of the mixture into mini candy parchment cups.
5. Refrigerate overnight.

Having chocolate cravings? This recipe has you covered. Again, if you prefer homemade chocolate sauce, this recipe will work just as well. It also works just as well if you substitute the stevia with another natural sweetener you're more accustomed to!

14. Fudgy Peanut Butter Cubes

Serves: 12
Prepping Time:
~5 min

**Nutritional
Information
(per serving)**

Calories: 313 kcal
Carbs: 5.5g
Fat: 30g
Protein: 5.1g
Fiber: 2.2g
Sugar: 2.4g

INGREDIENTS:

- 1 cup peanut butter.
- 1 cup coconut oil.
- ¼ cup almond milk (preferably vanilla flavored for taste).

Chocolate Sauce:
- ¼ cup cocoa powder
- 2 tablespoons coconut oil

Total number of ingredients: 5

METHOD:

1. Place coconut oil and peanut butter in a pot.
2. Melt on stove at low heat. Mix until smooth.
3. Place in a blender and add almond milk.
4. Blend until smooth.
5. Pour mixture into a non-stick loaf pan and refrigerate until firm (about 2 hours).
6. Combine ingredients for chocolate sauce.
7. Once peanut butter fudge is firm, drizzle chocolate sauce over fudge.

Are you busy? You can still keep your nutrition up to speed with this tasty and quick 5 ingredient recipe.

15. Vanilla Fat Bombs

Serves: 14
Prepping Time:
~15 min

Nutritional
Information
(per serving)

Calories: 137 kcal
Carbs: 1.4g
Fat: 14.1g
Protein: 0.7g
Fiber: 0.8g
Sugar: 0.5g

INGREDIENTS:

- 1 cup macadamia nuts.
- ½ cup coconut oil (or oil of your choice).
- 2 teaspoons vanilla extract.

Total number of ingredients: 3

METHOD:

1. Place all ingredients in a blender and blend until smooth.
2. Pour mixture into an ice tray and place in fridge until firm.

For those of you who love recipes with less ingredients and barely any effort involved you'll be sure to love this one! Three ingredients, high fat, low carb levels, and craving-satisfying!

16. Ginger Fat Bombs

Serves: 10
Prepping Time:
~5 min

___

Nutritional
Information
(per serving)

Calories: 137 kcal
Carbs: 2.7g
Fat: 13.7g
Protein: 0.8g
Fiber: 1.6g
Sugar: 0.8g

INGREDIENTS:

- ⅓ cup coconut butter.
- ⅓ cup coconut oil.
- ¼ cup shredded coconut, unsweetened.
- 1 teaspoon ginger powder.

Total number of ingredients: 4

METHOD:

1. In a bowl, mix all ingredients until smooth.
2. Pour mixture into molds (for example, ice cube trays).
3. Place in fridge to set.

Another recipe with fewer than five ingredients! Also, if you find the batter not sweet enough, add a teaspoon of natural sugar or your sweetener of choice.

17. Mint Chocolate Fudge

Serves: 16
Prepping Time:
~15 min

Nutritional
Information
(per serving)

Calories: 445 kcal
Carbs: 15.8g
Fat: 40.4g
Protein: 4.7g
Fiber: 1.2g
Sugar: 7.5g

INGREDIENTS:

- 1½ cups coconut oil, melted.
- 1¼ cups almond butter (or nut butter of choice).
- ½ cup favorite natural sugar or sweetener (all work just fine).
- ½ cup dried parsley flakes (crazy, right?!).
- 2 teaspoons vanilla extract.
- 1 teaspoon peppermint extract.
- 1 pinch of salt.
- 10 oz. melted dark chocolate (optional, again I use store bought).

Total number of ingredients: 8

METHOD:

1. Add all ingredients in a blender. Blend till smooth.
2. Pour into a nonstick pan and freeze until firm.
3. If adding chocolate, drizzle on top once the fudge is firm.
4. Keep refrigerated.

This recipe's secret ingredient? Dried parsley. It allows for the offset of flavoring and gives color without the use of artificial coloring.

CLEANSING LOW-CARB & PLANT-BASED RECIPES

1. Spicy Tofu Scramble

Serves: 1
Prepping Time:
~20 min

Nutritional
Information
(per serving)

Calories: 472 kcal
Carbs: 34.4g
Fat: 33.3g
Protein: 8.8g
Fiber: 15.1g
Sugar: 8.5g

INGREDIENTS:

- 1 onion, diced.
- ½ green pepper, diced.
- ½ cup mushrooms, chopped.
- 1 oz. package extra firm tofu, drained.
- 1 teaspoon curry powder.
- 1 tomato, chopped.
- 1 avocado, pitted and sliced.
- 1 teaspoon olive oil.
- 1 cup fresh spinach.
- 1 pinch pepper.

Total number of ingredients: 10

METHOD:

1. Sauté green peppers and onions in a skillet with olive oil for about 5 minutes.
2. Add in mushrooms.
3. Add dried tofu along with other spices and spinach.
4. Cook for about 10 minutes.
5. Place on a plate and top with sliced tomato and avocado.

When following a LCHF vegan diet, tofu is a great staple to have by your side. You can season it any way you like and its nutritional profile is perfect for your dietary needs.

2. Baked Green Beans

Serves: 3
Prepping Time:
~25 min

Nutritional
Information
(per serving)

Calories: 98 kcal
Carbs: 11.8g
Fat: 4.4g
Protein: 2.8g
Fiber: 7g
Sugar: 2.2g

INGREDIENTS:

- 1 lb. fresh green beans, end snipped.
- 3 tablespoons ground flax meal.
- 1 teaspoon salt.
- 1 pinch black pepper.
- 1 teaspoon olive oil.

Total number of ingredients: 5

METHOD:

1. Preheat oven to 350 °F.
2. Mix all ingredients in a bowl.
3. Place on a nonstick baking tray and bake for 20 to 25 minutes.

This is a life saver recipe, you guys. An entire pound of seasoned green beans is sure to fight off any hunger cravings you may be having!

3. Baked Eggplant with Tahini Dressing

Serves: 1
Prepping Time:
~20 min

___

Nutritional
Information
(per serving)

Calories: 446 kcal
Carbs: 50.4g
Fat: 22.6g
Protein: 8.9g
Fiber: 13.8g
Sugar: 21.8g

INGREDIENTS:

Part 1
- 1 eggplant, sliced.
- 1 clove garlic, minced.
- 1 tablespoon olive oil.
- 1 pinch salt.
- 1 pinch pepper.
- ½ **cup chopped parsley.**

Part 2
Sauce:
- 1 teaspoon olive oil.
- 1 onion, chopped.
- ½ **clove garlic, chopped.**
- 2 sprigs parsley, chopped.
- ⅓ cup almond milk.
- 1 teaspoon tahini.
- 1 pinch salt.

Total number of ingredients: 13

METHOD:

1. Preheat oven to 350 °F.
2. Mix all the ingredients from Part 1 into a bowl.
3. Place on a nonstick baking tray and bake for 30 minutes.
4. For the sauce, place all ingredients for the sauce in a blender.
5. Blend until smooth.

Eggplants can leave you completely satisfied for an entire meal. Talk about pure plant power!

4. Veggie Detox Soup

Serves: 6
Prepping Time:
~30 min

Nutritional
Information
(per serving)

Calories: 44 kcal
Carbs: 9.1g
Fat: 0.3g
Protein: 1.2g
Fiber: 2.5g
Sugar: 3.2g

INGREDIENTS:

- ½ cup lemon juice.
- 6 cups water.
- ½ onion, diced.
- 2 cloves garlic, minced.
- ½ cup celery, diced.
- 3 carrots, diced.
- ½ cup broccoli florets.
- 1 cup tomatoes, chopped.
- ¼ teaspoon cinnamon.
- salt and pepper to taste.
- 2 cups kale.

Total number of ingredients: 12

METHOD:

1. Sauté onions and garlic.
2. Add sautéed onions and garlic to a pot filled with boiling water and stir on medium heat.
3. Add remaining vegetables except kale and stir occasionally for 5 minutes.
4. Add spices and let simmer for 15 minutes.
5. Add kale and lemon and let simmer until all vegetables are soft.

The fiber contained in all these fresh veggies allows the net count of carbs to be less than 10g for an entire meal's serving. This soup is nothing but the best plant-powered medicine for you!

5. Spinach Pepper Quiche

**Serves: 6
Prepping Time:
~15 min**

**Nutritional
Information
(per serving)**

Calories: 98 kcal
Carbs: 11.4g
Fat: 1.9g
Protein: 9g
Fiber: 1.5g
Sugar: 1.5g

INGREDIENTS:

- 1 lb. extra firm tofu.
- 1 teaspoon onion powder.
- 1 teaspoon garlic powder.
- 1 pinch salt.
- ¼ cup cornstarch.
- ¼ cup nutritional yeast.
- 1 tablespoon Dijon mustard.
- 1 teaspoon lemon juice.
- 2 cups fresh spinach.
- 1 bell pepper, chopped.
- 2 teaspoons red pepper flakes.

Total number of ingredients: 11

METHOD:

1. Heat oven to 350 °F.
2. Lightly grease a shallow pie dish.
3. Place all ingredients, except spinach and pepper, in a blender. Blend until smooth.
4. Place mixture in a bowl.
5. Chop spinach.
6. Add chopped spinach and pepper to mixture from Step 4 and mix well.
7. Pour mixture into pie dish and bake for 45 minutes.

The fiber in the spinach comprises 2/3 of the carb content. This enables a low level of net carbs, around 11g per meal serving.

6. Tofu and Broccoli Filled Avocado

Serves: 2
Prepping Time:
~30 min

___

Nutritional
Information
(per serving
half avocado)

Calories: 290 kcal
Carbs: 10.6g
Fat: 27g
Protein: 2.1g
Fiber: 9.1g
Sugar: 1.5g

INGREDIENTS:

- 1 tablespoon Dijon mustard.
- ½ clove garlic, sliced.
- 3 tablespoons olive oil.
- 1 avocado, halved and pitted.
- 1 pinch chili flakes.
- 1 pinch salt and pepper.
- 1 pinch cumin.
- 2 tablespoons lemon juice.
- ⅓ package extra firm tofu, drained.
- 1 cup broccoli florets.

Total number of ingredients: 10

METHOD:

1. Prepare sauce by mixing lemon, mustard, olive oil, garlic and spices in a bowl.
2. In a separate bowl, pour mixture over broccoli and tofu cubes to marinate then place in fridge.
3. Grill avocado with olive oil, salt and pepper, then place marinated tofu and broccoli on grill.
4. Once charred, remove from grill.
5. Chop grilled tofu and broccoli, then spoon into avocado.

A great staple for LCHF vegans? Avocados. Extremely high in fat and fiber, equaling a low net carb count! More importantly? They're delicious!

7. Stuffed Portobello Mushrooms

Serves: 4
Prepping Time:
~15 min

___

Nutritional
Information
(per serving)

Calories: 120 kcal
Carbs: 11.5g
Fat: 7.1g
Protein: 2.6g
Fiber: 3g
Sugar: 5.8g

INGREDIENTS:

- 4 Portobello mushrooms.
- 2 tablespoons olive oil.
- 1 onion, diced.
- 1 zucchini, diced.
- 1 roasted red pepper, diced.
- 1 pinch each of the following spices: oregano, salt, black pepper and pepper flakes.
- 5 sundried tomatoes, diced.
- 3 cloves garlic, sliced.
- ¼ cup fresh spinach.
- Vegan cashew Parmesan (optional; this is extremely simple homemade).

Total number of ingredients: 12-13

METHOD:

1. Preheat oven to 350 °F.
2. Sauté all ingredients except cashew, then spoon into mushrooms.
3. If using cashew Parmesan, spread on top of each mushroom.
4. Place mushrooms in oven and bake for 45 minutes.

This recipe is great because you have the freedom to stuff and spice the mushrooms with whatever veggies, whole foods and spices you like!

8. Sesame Tofu with Eggplant

Serves: 4
Prepping Time:
~20 min

Nutritional
Information
(per serving)

Calories: 285 kcal
Carbs: 14.9g
Fat: 20.1g
Protein: 12g
Fiber: 6.1g
Sugar: 4.4g

INGREDIENTS:

- 1 lb. extra firm tofu, drained.
- 1 cup cilantro, chopped.
- 3 tablespoons rice vinegar.
- 2 cloves garlic, chopped.
- 1 eggplant, julienned.
- salt and pepper to taste.
- ¼ cup sesame seeds.
- ¼ cup of soy sauce, low sodium.
- 1 tablespoon red pepper flakes, crushed.
- 4 tablespoons sesame oil.

Total number of ingredients: 10

METHOD:

1. Preheat oven to 200 °F.
2. Place 2 tablespoons sesame oil and the cilantro, red pepper flakes, rice vinegar and garlic in a bowl and mix.
3. Cook eggplant in a lightly greased skillet until soft then add seasoned mix from Step 2.
4. In another skillet, add 2 tablespoons sesame oil and tofu and sauté until crisp.
5. Pour in the soy sauce and let tofu pieces soak in the soy sauce in order to appear caramelized.
6. Place tofu pieces on top of eggplant noodles and voila.

9. Zucchini Noodles with Avocado Pesto

Serves: 2
Prepping Time:
~15 min

Nutritional
Information
(per serving)

Calories: 234 kcal
Carbs: 17.3g
Fat: 16.2g
Protein: 5.8g
Fiber: 7.3g
Sugar: 6.3g

INGREDIENTS:

- 3 zucchinis, cut into very thin ribbons with a veggie peeler.
- salt and pepper to taste.
- 1 tablespoon olive oil.
- ½ avocado.
- 1 cup fresh basil.
- ¼ cup walnuts.
- 2 cloves garlic, chopped.
- ½ lemon.
- ¼ cup cashew cheese.
- ½ cup of water (only if needed to even out consistency).

Total number of ingredients: 10

METHOD:

1. Place ribboned zucchini in a bowl and toss with salt. Let sit.
2. Add avocado, basil, walnuts, lemon, garlic and parmesan cheese. Mix well and add water if needed.
3. Place zucchinis in a greased skillet and sauté for 5 minutes or until soft.
4. Pour dressing over zucchini and toss gently.

This pasta is the perfect go-to to cleanse your system and make you a powerhouse for the rest of the day. Have this meal on a day when you have a high level fat bomb to even out your nutrition levels!

10. Mushroom Tofu Lettuce Wraps

Serves: 2
Prepping Time:
~25 min

Nutritional
Information
(per serving)

Calories: 133 kcal
Carbs: 10.4g
Fat: 7.7g
Protein: 5.6g
Fiber: 6.1g
Sugar: 3.4g

INGREDIENTS:

- 1 oz. extra firm tofu.
- ½ avocado, pitted and peeled.
- ¾ lb. fresh mushrooms, chopped.
- lemon juice, to taste.
- salt and pepper.
- 3 cloves garlic, minced.
- soy sauce (optional).
- 2 lettuce leaves.

Total number of ingredients: 8

METHOD:

1. To a lightly greased skillet add garlic and mushrooms.
2. Cook for 5 minutes, then add tofu.
3. Mix thoroughly and add soy sauce (if desired) and spices.
4. Keep cooking until tofu is cooked through.
5. Place on a bed of lettuce and add lemon juice.
6. Garnish with avocado slices.

By having a dish that uses tofu instead of meat for your proteins and dietary needs, as well as lettuce instead of bread, you can ensure optimum health.

11. Cumin Cashew Cream

Serves: 1 cup
Prepping Time:
~4 min

Nutritional
Information
(per serving)

Calories: 510 kcal
Carbs: 33g
Fat: 37.5g
Protein: 25.5g
Fiber: 7.5g
Sugar: 9g

INGREDIENTS:

- 3 tablespoons nutritional yeast.
- ¾ cup raw cashews.
- ¼ teaspoon garlic powder.
- 1 teaspoon whole black peppercorns to taste
- 1 teaspoon cumin to taste
- ¾ teaspoon salt.

Total number of ingredients: 4

METHOD:

1. Mix all the ingredients with a food processor or blender

LOW-CARB & PLANT-BASED SMOOTHIES

1. Shamrock Smoothie

Serves: 2
Prepping Time:
~5 min

Nutritional
Information
(per serving)

Calories: 39 kcal
Carbs: 5.1g
Fat: 1.8g
Protein: 0.6g
Fiber: 3g
Sugar: 3.1g

INGREDIENTS:

- 2 cups water.
- ½ cup lettuce.
- ¼ cup pineapple, chopped.
- ½ cup cucumber, peeled and sliced.
- ¼ cup kiwi, peeled and chopped.
- ¼ cup avocado, peeled and pitted.
- 3 tablespoons stevia.

Total number of ingredients: 7

METHOD:

1. Blend all ingredients together in a blender. Add more or less of what you prefer.

2. The Ultimate Green Smoothie

Serves: 2
Prepping Time:
~5 min

Nutritional
Information
(per serving)

Calories: 104 kcal
Carbs: 8g
Fat: 7.1g
Protein: 2g
Fiber: 4.9g
Sugar: 1.9g

INGREDIENTS:

- 2 cups spinach.
- ½ avocado, pitted and peeled.
- ½ cucumber.
- ½ cup parsley.
- 1 cup water.
- ice cubes (optional).

Total number of ingredients: 6

METHOD:

1. Blend all ingredients together in a blender. Add more or less of what you prefer.

3. Nutty Green Smoothie

Serves: 2
Prepping Time:
~5 min

Nutritional
Information
(per serving)

Calories: 212 kcal
Carbs: 9.1g
Fat: 16.6g
Protein: 2.9g
Fiber: 4.4g
Sugar: 2.7g

INGREDIENTS:

- ¼ cup coconut milk.
- ½ avocado, pitted and peeled.
- ½ cup water.
- ½ cup fresh mint.
- 2 tablespoons pistachios.
- 1 tablespoon vanilla extract.
- 2 drops stevia.
- ¼ cup spinach.

Total number of ingredients: 8

METHOD:

1. Blend all ingredients together in a blender. Add more or less of what you prefer.

A popular favorite! ... and look at the nutritional value of it! A 17g fat content!

4. Coconut Berry Smoothie

Serves: 3
Prepping Time:
~5 min

___

Nutritional
Information
(per serving)

Calories: 166 kcal
Carbs: 14.7g
Fat: 10.5g
Protein: 3.6g
Fiber: 2.5g
Sugar: 7.5g

INGREDIENTS:

- ¾ cup frozen blueberries (or your choice of berries).
- ¾ cup almond milk.
- 2 tablespoons ground chia seeds.
- 2 tablespoons coconut oil.
- 3 drops stevia.

Total number of ingredients: 5

METHOD:

1. Blend all ingredients in a blender in a blender. Add more or less of what you prefer.

5. Fruity Chocolaty Avocado Smoothie

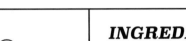

Serves: 2
Prepping Time:
~5 min

Nutritional
Information
(per serving)

Calories: 138 kcal
Carbs: 20.5g
Fat: 4.4g
Protein: 3.0g
Fiber: 3.35g
Sugar: 13g

INGREDIENTS:

- ½ cup cashew flavored almond milk.
- ¼ avocado, pitted and peeled.
- ⅓ cup frozen raspberries.
- 1 tablespoon cocoa powder

Total number of ingredients: 4

METHOD:

1. Blend all ingredients together in a blender. Add more or less of what you prefer.

6. Chocolate Lover's Smoothie

Serves: 1
Prepping Time:
~5 min

Nutritional
Information
(per serving)

Calories: 232 kcal
Carbs: 9.2g
Fat: 19g
Protein: 3.8g
Fiber: 0.6g
Sugar: 2.9g

INGREDIENTS:

- 1 teaspoon vanilla extract.
- 1 teaspoon almond butter.
- ¼ cup coconut milk.
- ¼ cup water.
- ¼ cup cocoa powder.
- a few dark chocolate chip chunks (optional).

Total number of ingredients: 6

METHOD:

1. Blend all ingredients together in a blender. Add more or less of what you prefer.

7. Strawberry Chocolate Milkshake

Serves: 2
Prepping Time:
~5 min

Nutritional
Information
(per serving)

Calories: 313 kcal
Carbs: 11.5g
Fat: 28.1g
Protein: 3.6g
Fiber: 1g
Sugar: 6g

INGREDIENTS:

- 1 cup coconut milk.
- ½ cup fresh strawberries.
- 3 drops stevia.
- ¼ cup cocoa powder.
- ice cubes (optional, for thicker consistency).

Total number of ingredients: 5

METHOD:

1. Blend all ingredients together in a blender. Add more or less of what you prefer.

The coconut milk acts as a great nutritional substitute for regular milk by having a great fat to carb ratio per cup. Also, you can't go wrong with the simplicity of a 5 ingredient smoothie!

8. Raspberry Avocado Smoothie

Serves: 2
Prepping Time:
~5 min

Nutritional
Information
(per serving)

Calories: 212 kcal
Carbs: 9.1g
Fat: 16.6g
Protein: 2.9g
Fiber: 4.4g
Sugar: 2.7g

INGREDIENTS:

- ¼ cup coconut milk.
- ½ avocado, pitted and peeled.
- ½ cup water.
- ½ cup fresh mint.
- 2 tablespoons pistachios.
- 1 tablespoon vanilla extract.
- 2 drops of stevia.
- ¼ cup spinach.

Total number of ingredients: 8

METHOD:

1. Blend all ingredients together in a blender. Add more or less of what you prefer.

9. Pumpkin Acai Bowl

Serves: 1
Prepping Time:
~10 min

Nutritional
Information
(per serving)

Calories: 1300 kcal
Carbs: 75.3g
Fat: 96.5g
Protein: 32.3g
Fiber: 3.1g
Sugar: 26.5g

INGREDIENTS:

- ¼ cup pumpkin puree (optional)
- 1 cup almonds.
- 1 pinch cinnamon.
- 2 tablespoons pistachios.
- ¼ cup blackberries (or berry of your choice).
- 1 tablespoon cocoa powder.
- ½ avocado, pitted and peeled.
- 1 banana, sliced.

Total number of ingredients: 8

METHOD:

1. Blend together cocoa powder, avocado, pumpkin puree, some of the berries and the cinnamon in a blender until smooth.
2. Pour mixture into a serving bowl and top with leftover berries, nuts and banana.

10. PB&G Smoothie

Serves: 1
Prepping Time:
~5 min

_____

Nutritional
Information
(per serving)

Calories: 189 kcal
Carbs: 5.4g
Fat: 8.3g
Protein: 4.5g
Fiber: 3.6g
Sugar: 9.6g

INGREDIENTS:

- 1 cup spinach.
- 1 tablespoon peanut butter.
- 2 drops stevia.
- water (depending on the desired consistency).
- 1 tablespoon cocoa powder.

Total number of ingredients: 5

METHOD:

1. Blend all ingredients together in a blender. Add more or less of what you prefer.

The peanut butter and green smoothie is a favorite. Do you want a plant based, green smoothie which has a thick, creamy and sweet taste? This is the way to go.

LOW-CARB VEGAN SALADS

1. Tofu Broccoli Salad

Serves: 2
Prepping Time:
~15 min

Nutritional
Information
(per serving)

Calories: 395 kcal
Carbs: 19.4g
Fat: 31.3g
Protein: 9.1g
Fiber: 3.9g
Sugar: 2.5g

INGREDIENTS:

For the Sause
- ¼ cup tahini.
- 2 cloves garlic, minced.
- juice of 1 lemon.
- 1 tablespoon sesame oil.
- 2 tablespoons rice wine vinegar.

For the Salad
- 1 head broccoli, cut in florets.
- 1 tablespoon walnuts, halved.
- 1 oz. extra firm tofu.
- 2 cups packaged mixed greens (or make your own).
- 1 tablespoon olive oil.

Total number of ingredients: 10

METHOD:

1. Blend all the sauce ingredients together in a blender. Add more or less of what you prefer.
2. Sauté tofu in a greased pan, add spices and stir occasionally until done.
3. Add broccoli to pan and sauté in olive oil until tender.
4. Place tofu in a bowl and add the mixed greens, dressing and nuts. Enjoy!

2. Chickpeas and Greens Salad

Serves: 4
Prepping Time:
~15 min

Nutritional
Information
(per serving)

Calories: 166 kcal
Carbs: 20g
Fat: 6.8g
Protein: 6.1g
Fiber: 5.3g
Sugar: 0.4g

INGREDIENTS:

- ½ cup kale.
- ¾ cup brocoli florets.
- 1 cup chickpeas, cooked.
- 4 tablespoons hummus (store bought or homemade).
- 2 tablespoons sesame seeds.
- 3 tablespoons pumpkin seeds.

Total number of ingredients: 6

METHOD:

1. Steam the kale and broccoli.
2. Once done, place in a bowl.
3. Add chickpeas, sesame seeds and pumpkin seeds. Mix well.
4. Portion onto 4 plates.
5. Top each plate with a tablespoon of hummus..

3. Avocado Kale Salad

Serves: 4
Prepping Time:
~15 min

Nutritional
Information
(per serving)

Calories: 290 kcal
Carbs: 17.1g
Fat: 22.5g
Protein: 4.9g
Fiber: 9.5g
Sugar: 3.4g

INGREDIENTS:

Salad:
- 1 ½ avocados, chopped.
- ½ onion, sliced.
- ½ cucumber, sliced.
- 1 cup kale, chopped.
- 1 red chili (optional), sliced.

Dressing:
- 2 tablespoons lemon juice.
- 1 avocado.
- 1 teaspoon cayenne pepper.
- 1 pinch of salt.
- 1 pinch of pepper.
- ¼ cup chopped almonds (or nuts of your choice for topping).

Total number of ingredients: 11

METHOD:

1. Place all the ingredients for the salad in a bowl and toss.
2. Blend all the dressing ingredients together except the almonds.
3. Pour dressing over salad and toss.
4. Add chopped almonds on top.

4. Tabbouleh

Serves: 6
Prepping Time:
~30 min

Nutritional
Information
(per serving)

Calories: 183 kcal
Carbs: 5.4g
Fat: 17.7g
Protein: 0.6g
Fiber: 1.1g
Sugar: 2.5g

INGREDIENTS:

- ½ cup lemon juice.
- ½ cup olive oil.
- 1 onion, chopped.
- 10 sprigs parsley, chopped.
- 2 cups tomatoes, chopped.
- salt and pepper to taste.

Total number of ingredients: 7

METHOD:

1. In a bowl, mix parsley, tomatoes and onions.
2. Gradually top with lemon juice, olive oil, salt and pepper and mix.
3. Keep mixing, tasting, and adding until preferred taste is achieved.

Mediterranean cuisine can be a bit tricky when it comes to a keto vegan diet; however, their salads never disappoint. Tabbouleh is usually a side salad complimenting whatever else you may be eating.

5. Nut Broccoli Salad

Serves: 6
Prepping Time:
~15 min

Nutritional
Information
(per serving)

Calories: 349 kcal
Carbs: 17.5g
Fat: 26.4g
Protein: 10.3g
Fiber: 6.2g
Sugar: 6.2g

INGREDIENTS:

Salad:
- 5 cups broccoli.
- 2 cups shredded carrots.
- ½ cup walnuts.
- ½ cup roasted peanuts.
- ¼ cup onion, chopped.

Sauce:
- ½ cup peanut butter.
- Siracha (optional).
- salt and pepper to taste.
- 2 tablespoons coconut oil.
- juice of ½ a lemon.
- 2 tablespoons soy sauce.
- 1 teaspoon rice vinegar.

Total number of ingredients: 12

METHOD:

1. Mix all the salad ingredients in a bowl.
2. In a separate bowl, mix together the dressing ingredients until smooth.
3. Pour dressing over salad and mix until evenly coated
4. Refrigerate to let all the flavors soak in, then serve!

6. Fattoush

INGREDIENTS:

Salad:
- 1 pita bread (will be used for the bread crisps in the fattoush; you can use more or less depending on dietary preference).
- salt and pepper to taste.
- 1 head lettuce, chopped.
- 1 cucumber, chopped.
- 3 tomatoes, chopped.
- 3 onions, chopped.
- ½ **teaspoon sumac.**
- 4 radishes, sliced.
- 1 cup parsley, chopped.
- 1 teaspoon olive oil.

Lemon-Vinaigrette Sauce:
- juice of 1 lemon.
- ⅓ cup olive oil.
- 1 teaspoon sumac.
- salt and pepper to taste.
- ½ teaspoon ground cinnamon.

Total number of ingredients: 16

METHOD:

1. Toast pita bread until crisp, break, and place in oiled skillet until browned.
2. Add salt, pepper and sumac.
3. In a mixing bowl, mix the tomatoes, onions, cucumber, radish, lettuce and parsley.
4. For the dressing, mix all the dressing ingredients in a small bowl.
5. Mix dressing with salad and toss, then add the pita chips and toss a bit more.

Serves: 6
Prepping Time:
~20 min

Nutritional
Information
(per serving)

Calories: 194 kcal
Carbs: 15.5g
Fat: 13.3g
Protein: 2.7g
Fiber: 3.9g
Sugar: 4.8g

7. Mixed Greens with Raspberry Vinaigrette

Serves: 1
Prepping Time:
~5 min

Nutritional
Information
(per serving)

Calories: 937 kcal
Carbs: 17.7g
Fat: 95.4g
Protein: 8.1g
Fiber: 4.9g
Sugar: 9.1g

INGREDIENTS:

Salad:
- ½ cup mixed greens.
- 3 tablespoons pine nuts, roasted.
- 2 tablespoons homemade cumin cashew cream.
- salt and ground pepper to taste.

Vinaigrette:
- ⅓ cup white wine vinegar.
- ⅓ cup fresh raspberries.
- ⅓ cup olive oil.

Total number of ingredients: 8

METHOD:

1. Mix all salad ingredients together,
2. Blend dressing ingredients in a blender, then pour through a fine strainer into a cup to remove thick clumps.
3. Top salad with vinaigrette and enjoy!

8. Crumbled Broccoli Tofu Salad

Serves: 1
Prepping Time:
~5 min

Nutritional
Information
(per serving)

Calories: 232 kcal
Carbs: 22.3g
Fat: 10.1g
Protein: 12.6g
Fiber: 4.8g
Sugar: 8g

INGREDIENTS:

- ½ cup tofu (4oz).
- ½ head broccoli florets.
- 1 onion, chopped.
- 1 clove garlic, chopped.
- 2 teaspoons soy sauce.
- 1 teaspoon sesame seed oil.
- 2 teaspoons sesame seeds.
- salt and pepper to taste.

Total number of ingredients: 9

METHOD:

1. Steam broccoli and tofu in a pot.
2. Once done, rinse under cold water and put broccoli in a separate bowl.
3. Dry the tofu as much as possible by patting with a towel, then crumble and add in the bowl containing the broccoli (keep them separated in the bowl).
4. Add the garlic, onions and ½ the soy sauce over the tofu only, and let soak for 5 minutes.
5. Add the rest of the soy sauce, sesame seeds and oil over both items.
6. Toss gently and add pepper and salt if desired.

9. Baby Kale Topped with Raspberry and Pecans

Serves: 4
Prepping Time:
~15 min

Nutritional
Information
(per serving)

Calories: 294 kcal
Carbs: 8.2g
Fat: 27.7g
Protein: 3.7g
Fiber: 3.3g
Sugar: 2.6g

INGREDIENTS:

Salad:
- 1 cup raw pecans.
- 6 drops stevia.
- ¾ cup baby kale.
- handful of raspberries (about a ¼ cup).

Maple Vinaigrette:
- 2 tablespoons olive oil.
- 2 tablespoons balsamic vinegar.
- 1 drop stevia or teaspoon maple syrup.
- 1 clove garlic, minced.
- salt and pepper to taste.
- 2 teaspoons Dijon Mustard.
- 2 teaspoons lemon juice.

Total number of ingredients: 12

METHOD:

1. Preheat oven to 350 °F.
2. In a bowl mix the pecans and stevia then place on a baking sheet and bake for 10 minutes.
3. Mix the ingredients for the vinaigrette in a bowl.
4. Place the kale in a bowl and add the pecans, raspberries and vinaigrette.

10. Avocado Mexican Salad

Serves: 4
Prepping Time:
~15 min

Nutritional
Information
(per serving)

Calories: 115 kcal
Carbs: 7.6g
Fat: 8.7g
Protein: 1.5g
Fiber: 4.7g
Sugar: 2.8g

INGREDIENTS:

- ½ tablespoon olive oil.
- 1 pinch of salt and 1 pinch of pepper to taste.
- 1 teaspoon red wine vinegar.
- ¼ onion, chopped.
- 1 tablespoon fresh cilantro, chopped.
- 1 ripe avocado.
- ¼ head lettuce, chopped.
- ½ jalapeno, chopped.
- 12 cherry tomatoes, quartered.

Total number of ingredients: 10

METHOD:

1. Combine oil, vinegar, tomatoes, salt and pepper in a bowl and let sit for an hour.
2. Add jalapeño, onion and cilantro and toss.
3. Place chopped lettuce and sliced avocados on a plate and spoon the mixture from Step 2 on top.

DESSERTS

1. 2-Minute Microwave Cinnamon Pecan Bread

Serves: 4
Prepping Time:
~5 min

Nutritional
Information
(per serving:
1 mini loaf)

Calories: 125 kcal
Carbs: 3.2g
Fat: 11.3g
Protein: 3g
Fiber: 2.3g
Sugar: 1.1g

INGREDIENTS:

- ⅓ cup almond flour (or any nut flour of your preference).
- 1 flax egg.
- ½ teaspoon baking powder.
- ¼ teaspoon salt.
- ¼ teaspoon cinnamon (optional).
- ¼ cup chopped pecans.

Total number of ingredients: 6

METHOD:

1. In a bowl, add the almond flour, baking powder, cinnamon and salt and thoroughly mix.
2. Add the flax egg and pecans and stir until evenly mixed.
3. Lightly oil (using olive oil) a cup big enough to fit the batter.
4. Pour the mixture into the cup and microwave for about 2 minutes or until firm.
5. Slice the mini loaf into about 4 or 5 pieces.
6. Toast the slices if you want.

2. Banana Nut Bread

Serves: 10
Prepping Time:
~10 min

Nutritional
Information
(per serving)

Calories: 249 kcal
Carbs: 11.8g
Fat: 20.4g
Protein: 4.3g
Sugar: 19g

INGREDIENTS:

- 3 bananas, chopped.
- 3 flax eggs.
- 2 cups almond flour or oatmeal.
- ⅓ cup walnuts (or any other keto friendly nut you prefer).
- ¼ cup coconut oil or olive oil (depending on availability or preference).
- ½ teaspoon baking powder.

Total number of ingredients: 6

METHOD:

1. Preheat oven to 350 °F.
2. Minimally grease a loaf pan with whichever oil you chose.
3. Add all the ingredients into one bowl and mix well.
4. Pour the mix into loaf pan.
5. Cook for 1 hour at 350 °F or until done.

Craving that natural sweet, sugary taste that comes from bananas? This banana bread recipe comes with a twist as it has walnuts, which give an extra spin to the normal banana bread! Also, the walnuts contribute 5.9g protein per slice. Indulge your sweet tooth with a dessert that contains half the carbs and sugar of a normal sweet loaf!

3. Almond Maple Crumble Dessert Loaf

Serves: 8
Prepping Time:
~15 min

___

Nutritional
Information
(per serving)

Calories: 178 kcal
Carbs: 6g
Fat: 14.9g
Protein: 6.3g
Fiber: 2.8g
Sugar: 1.8g

INGREDIENTS:

- 1½ cups almond flour (or any other nut flour).
- 4 flax eggs.
- ¼ cup finely ground flaxseed.
- 1 tablespoon whole flaxseed (optional).
- 2 tablespoons crushed almonds (optional).
- ½ teaspoon salt.
- ½ teaspoon baking soda.
- ½ teaspoon apple cider vinegar.
- 2 drops stevia.

Total number of ingredients: 9

METHOD:

1. Preheat the oven to 300 °F.
2. Lightly grease a loaf pan with olive oil.
3. Add all the ingredients in a bowl and mix well.
4. Pour the batter into greased loaf pan.
5. Bake for about 45 minutes or until a knife comes out of the center clean.
6. Remove from oven and let cool completely before slicing.

The small splash of sweetener and apple cider vinegar allows for the most perfect, sweetened combination, sure to have you coming back for another slice, and that's okay because this dessert is supportive of your carb and sugar restrictions! By taking a slice to satisfy that sweet tooth, you barely add on to your daily carb count with 6g per slice!

4. Dark Chocolate Raspberry Cups

Serves: 14
Prepping Time:
~20 min

Nutritional
Information
(per serving)

Calories: 222 kcal
Carbs: 3.4g
Fat: 21.6g
Protein: 3.7g
Fiber: 0.6g
Sugar: 0.3g

INGREDIENTS:

Chocolate:
- 1 cup dairy free, sugar free dark chocolate (store bought).
- ½ cup cocoa butter.
- 2 tablespoons coconut oil.
- 1 teaspoon vanilla extract.

Fruit Topping:
- 1 ½ cups raspberries (fresh or frozen).
- 25 almonds (roasted for about 5 minutes).

Total number of ingredients: 6

METHOD:

1. Place one almond in each raspberry.
2. Space each almond-raspberry on a tray and freeze for about an hour.
3. Place all the chocolate ingredients into a pot over low heat and stir constantly until everything is mixed.
4. Pour the chocolate sauce into individual mini cupcake molds. At about midway mark, place 1-2 almond-raspberries, then cover with a bit more chocolate sauce
5. Place in the fridge for about 30 minutes or until firm.

If you have not tried a raspberry and chocolate combination, you have not tasted the perfect fruity sweet! These are great as an evening snack or before heading out of the house. With 21.6g of fat they are sure to satisfy your dietary needs as well.

5. Pumpkin Pie Bites

Serves: 15
Prepping Time:
~20 min

Nutritional
Information
(per serving)

Calories: 124 kcal
Carbs: 2.3g
Fat: 12.4g
Protein: 0.7g
Fiber: 2.0g
Sugar: 0.7g

INGREDIENTS:

- ½ cup pumpkin puree.
- 3 drops stevia.
- ¼ cup coconut butter, softened.
- ½ cup coconut oil, melted.
- 2 teaspoons cinnamon.
- ½ cup pecans.

Total number of ingredients: 6

METHOD:

1. Combine the pumpkin puree, coconut oil and coconut butter in a bowl.
2. Stir in the sweetener and the cinnamon.
3. Mix together evenly and pour into mini molds or an ice cube tray.
4. Refrigerate until firm.

If you are a pumpkin lover, then you are sure to love this recipe! To keep it simple, ensure that you use a premade vegan, fresh pumpkin puree for best results! Or if you're up for the task, use a homemade version.

6. Peanut Butter Brownies

Serves: 8
Prepping Time:
~15 min

Nutritional
Information
(per serving)

Calories: 142 kcal
Carbs: 6g
Fat: 8.8g
Protein: 10.2g
Fiber: 2.7g
Sugar: 1.9g

INGREDIENTS:

- 1½ cups water (room temperature).
- ½ cup peanut butter.
- ¼ cup cocoa powder.
- 6 drops stevia.
- 2 tablespoons coconut flour.
- 2 teaspoons baking powder.
- 2 scoops vegan protein powder of your choice (this recipe uses Vega chocolate flavored protein powder).

Total number of ingredients: 7

METHOD:

1. Preheat oven to 350 °F.
2. In a bowl, mix the warm water, stevia and peanut butter.
3. In a separate bowl, mix the cocoa powder, baking powder, Vega protein powder and coconut flour.
4. Add the mixture from Step 2 to that of Step 3 and mix well.
5. Pour batter into a slightly greased pan and let bake for 40-45 minutes, or until a knife comes out of the center clean.

7. Chocolate Covered Strawberries

Serves: 16
Prepping Time:
~20 min

Nutritional
Information
(per serving:
4 Strawberries)

Calories: 119 kcal
Carbs: 5.4g
Fat: 9.7g
Protein: 3.1g
Fiber: 0.5g
Sugar: 2.4g

INGREDIENTS:

- 16 Strawberries
- ¼ of 10 oz. milk-free and sugar-free dark chocolate bar

Total number of ingredients: 2

METHOD:

1. Melt the chocolate in a pot until it turns liquid. Once liquid, keep stirring.
2. Remove from heat and allow to cool and thicken.
3. Dip strawberries in the cooled chocolate, then place them on a parchment-lined tray.
4. Place in the fridge for about an hour or until chocolate is perfectly set.

A simple, tasty treat sure to satisfy any chocolate fruity cravings while still being ketogenic and vegan due to the sugar free, milk free chocolate utilized.

8. Keto-Vegan Chocolate Mousse

Serves: 16
Prepping Time:
~20 min

___

Nutritional
Information
(per serving)

Calories: 470 kcal
Carbs: 12.8g
Fat: 41.3g
Protein: 5.1g
Fiber: 0.4g
Sugar: 4.6g

INGREDIENTS:

- 1 can coconut milk
- 5-10 drops stevia
- 3 tablespoons coconut oil
- ½ cup cocoa powder
- 2 flax eggs
- 1 teaspoon vanilla

Total number of ingredients: 6

METHOD:

1. Pour ½ of the coconut milk into a pot and add the stevia. Mix until everything is dissolved.
2. Add the rest of the ingredients in a blender and blend well.
3. Pour the coconut milk and stevia mixture into the blender and blend again.
4. Pour the chocolate mousse into three separate jars and enjoy.

There are so many online adaptations of a delicious, fluffy, chocolate mousse. Thanks to the stevia and flax eggs this recipe serves your cravings while remaining keto vegan.

9. White Chocolate Raspberry Chocolate Chip Squares

Serves: 16
Prepping Time:
~20 min

Nutritional
Information
(per serving:
4 Strawberries)

Calories: 94 kcal
Carbs: 1.2g
Fat: 9.7g
Protein: 0.5g
Fiber: 0.4g
Sugar: 0.2g

INGREDIENTS:

- ¼ cup coconut oil
- ½ cup cocoa butter
- 1 teaspoon vanilla extract
- 1 teaspoon salt
- ½ cup fresh raspberries
- ¼ cup store bought dairy free, sugar free chocolate chips

Total number of ingredients: 6

METHOD:

1. Add a bit of water to a pan on medium heat.
2. Add cocoa butter and stir until it melts.
3. Add mix coconut oil, vanilla extract and salt and stir well.
4. Remove mixture from pan and place in blender.
5. Blend on high speed for 45 seconds
6. Evenly place half of the raspberries and chocolate chips on a parchment lined tray.
7. Pour the mixture from Step 5 on top.
8. Add the remaining raspberries and chocolate chips on top.
9. Freeze for about 15 minutes, or until hardened, and break into serving sized pieces.

10. Almond Joy Squares

Serves: 15
Prepping Time:
~20 min

Nutritional
Information
(per serving)

Calories: 262 kcal
Carbs: 5.9g
Fat: 25.4g
Protein: 2.5g
Fiber: 1.0g
Sugar: 1g

INGREDIENTS:

Chocolate Base:
- ½ cup coconut oil.
- ½ cup almond butter.
- 1 teaspoon stevia.
- 6 tablespoons cocoa powder.
- 2 teaspoons vanilla powder.

Coconut Top:
- 1 ⅓ cup shredded coconut, unsweetened.
- 6 tablespoons coconut oil.
- 1½ teaspoons vanilla extract.
- 15 almond halves.

Total number of ingredients: 9

METHOD:

1. For the topping, melt coconut oil and almond butter on low heat, then add all the other chocolate base ingredients except the vanilla. Mix well.
2. Once the mixture has thickened, stir in the vanilla.
3. Pour the mixture on a nonstick tray and place in the freezer.
4. For the coconut top; melt the coconut oil in a pan and stir in the coconut shreds.
5. Add the remaining coconut top ingredients and stir until it thickens.
6. Gently place the coconut mixture on top of the hardened chocolate.
7. Space the almonds on top of the coconut mixture, and place in fridge.

Missing that high sugar, artificial candy bar? Here's a healthy, low carb, low sugar, energy packed alternative!

CONCLUSION

I would like to thank you for purchasing this book and taking the time to read it.

I do hope that it has been helpful and that you found the information contained within the sections useful!

The Ketogenic Vegan diet is beneficial to your health and stamina. The combination of the two is the best thing you can do for your physical and mental well-being. Try it and you will be an ardent follower for life.

Keep in mind that you are not limited to the diet plan and recipes provided in this book! Keep on exploring until you create your very own culinary masterpiece!

Stay healthy and stay safe!

BONUS REMINDER

Don't forget to grab <u>your copy</u> of **'The Vegan Cookbook'**

By subscribing to our newsletter, you will receive the latest vegan recipes, plant-based cooking articles that make your mouth water and detailed ketogenic vegan information right in your inbox.

We also offer you a unique opportunity to read future vegan cookbooks for absolutely free...

Get your hands on our free vegan recipes and instant access to 'The Vegan Cookbook'.

Subscribe to the vegan newsletter and grab your copy here at

http://happyhealthygreen.life/vegan-newsletter

Enter your email address to get instant access. Support the vegan movement and say NO to animal cruelty!
We don't like spam and understand you don't like spam either. We'll email you no more than 2 times per week.

THANK YOU

Finally, if you enjoyed this book, then we would like to ask you for a small favor. Would you be kind enough to leave an honest review for this book? It'd be greatly appreciated by both the future reader and me!

You can send us your feedback here:
http://happyhealthygreen.life/about-us/evahammond/low-carb-vegan-review

Did you discover any grammar mistakes, confusing explanations or wrongful information?
Don't hesitate to send us an email! You can reach us at info@happyhealthygreen.life

We promise to get back at you as soon as time allows us. If this book requires a revision, we'll send you the updated eBook for free after the revised book is available.

SOURCES

http://ajcn.nutrition.org/content/85/1/238.full

http://sciencedrivennutrition.com/the-ketogenic-diet/

http://theconversation.com/what-are-ketogenic-diets-can-they-treat-epilepsy-and-brain-cancer-83401

http://www.healthline.com/nutrition/23-studies-on-low-carb-and-low-fat-diets#section9

http://www.medicalnewstoday.com/articles/319287.php

http://www.sandiegouniontribune.com/business/biotech/sd-me-ketogenic-health-20170905-story.html

https://draxe.com/keto-diet-food-list/

https://globenewswire.com/news-release/2017/08/29/1101488/0/en/Weight-Loss-Doctor-Nishant-Rao-Improves-Upon-the-Ketogenic-Diet-for-More-Consistent-Results.html

https://www.aocs.org/stay-informed/read-inform/featured-articles/prescribing-dietary-fat-therapeutic-uses-of-ketogenic-diets-february-2016

https://www.dietdoctor.com/low-carb/keto

https://www.ncbi.nlm.nih.gov/pmc/articles/PMC2716748/

https://www.ncbi.nlm.nih.gov/pmc/articles/PMC2902940/

https://www.ncbi.nlm.nih.gov/pmc/articles/PMC3826507/

https://www.ncbi.nlm.nih.gov/pubmed/17447017

https://www.ncbi.nlm.nih.gov/pubmed/22673594

The Ketogenic Diet: A Complete Guide for the Dieter and Practitioner By Lyle McDonald https://books.google.co.ke/books?id=JtCZBe-2XVIC&pg=PA101&lpg=PA101&dq=medical+findings+on+macronutrients+in+ketogenic+diet&source=bl&ots=dPINf4CRDB&sig=O6oxDuSjYOd81Pff11lJ-LUImME&hl=en&sa=X&redir_esc=y#v=onepage&q=medical%20findings%20on%20macronutrients%20in%20ketogenic%20diet&f=false

www.mdpi.com/2072-6643/9/5/517/pdf

Manufactured by Amazon.ca
Bolton, ON